THE LEAD GENERATION GUIDE

The Five-Step Marketing System
To Attract Your Ideal Clients
& Increase Your Sales

GARY DAS

Copyright © 2023 Gary Das

All rights reserved. No part of this book may be reproduced or used in any manner without the prior written permission of the copyright owner, except for the use of brief quotations in a book review.

To request permissions, contact the publisher at team@garydas.com

The information in this book was correct at the time of publication, but the author does not assume any liability for loss or damage caused by errors or omissions.

ISBN: 9798362569969

Imprint: Independently published

PRAISE

The book gives a great insight in to the possibilities of growth within the industry and how individuals and firms can take back the reigns and build their own funnel of leads, target their niche and specialisms, and maintain ownership of their database. It gives a great introduction to multiple social media strategies and also the mindset behind the sales and consumer buying process.

- Vishal Viyas | London Mortgage Partners

The Lead Generation Guide gives a comprehensive overview of the key marketing principles that will bring a flood of new customers into your business. These principles work in any industry and will be valuable to both new and experienced business owners. If you implement the contents of this book, you'll never hear yourself say "I just need more leads" ever again.

- John Robery | Direct Response Copywriter

Gary's book has great insights that can help you navigate through gaining quality leads. Also, a helpful guide for self-improvement. Great book to read no matter what stage of your career you are at!

- Steve Collins | Trulife Mortgages & Protection

Just finished reading your book! Brilliant. I've spent over two years in the online business world, watching and listening to coaches telling me bits and pieces about online marketing and now it all makes sense.

The jigsaw pieces are all in place and I now have a clear understanding of the process I need to follow to attract and sell to my ideal client.

I'm a logical person and like an easy to follow, step by step approach to getting something done. Your book provides this and shows me how all the steps come together.

- Michaela Thorn | The Accounts Lady

If you're looking for proven techniques to scale your start-up at a low cost, you've found the perfect book. This is an incredible resource to add to your collection. I have no problem in recommending this book to entrepreneurs who are serious about scaling, especially using social media. Well done, Gary.

- Jade Bartholomew | Director at Sierra Six Media Limited

I helped Gary edit this book and I honestly didn't realise that my business was in dire need of the advice inside until I was already working on it. It's full of actionable marketing strategies and I've started implementing his system to help scale my business. Gary is a talented writer and I look forward to seeing what he writes next.

- Emily Williams | Copywriter & Editor at Emily Williams Writes

CONTENTS

Introduction	1
Basic Business & Marketing Principles	12
The Lead Generation Method	26
Step 1: Gaining Clarity	28
Step 2: Creating Content	51
Step 3: Social Media	70
Step 4: Marketing Techniques	92
Step 5: Sales Strategies	119
Summary	129
What to Do Next	131
About the Author	133

Introduction

Imagine you're standing in the middle of Oxford Street in London... blindfolded. (Don't worry, it's not that weird; this is about business, I promise.)

Hordes of people are going about their day, in true London style, at 100mph. Some are browsing during their lunch break; some are shopping with a purpose; others are there for a spot of mild entertainment.

Except you.

You're stood there, shouting at the top of your lungs about your business, hoping to capture the attention of a passer-by.

Now, let's pretend you do (miraculously) capture the attention of someone who happens to resonate with what you have to say.

Your job now is to turn their attention into a sale. But remember – you're blindfolded, so you know nothing about them other than the faint scent of body odour meeting your nostrils on this sweltering summer's day.

How successful do you think you'd be at converting them into a client?

My guess is that you've got more chance of selling snow to an Inuit.

So, why am I giving you this ridiculous example?

Well, it's simple. This is exactly how a lot of businesses are marketing online. They're blindly shouting their message to all and sundry, hoping someone relevant will hear it.

I see it time and time again when I start a coaching relationship with a business owner. I ask them to describe their ideal client to me and I'm either met by a blank face or a few random demographic descriptors.

It's amazing how quickly we can move the needle on their marketing by fleshing out a deep and clear client avatar for their business.

First, we choose a niche to focus on

I understand people don't like to do this because they feel like they're missing out, but jeepers. Even billion-pound companies with a marketing budget capable of reaching millions of people have a niche.

- Tesla started with electric cars
- Amazon started by only selling books
- Tony Robbins started with phobias
- Gucci started with equestrian leather goods
- The Buy To Let Business (now named Dynamo) started with *only* Buy To lets.

It's better to be everything to one person than nothing to millions. It's the fastest way to gain traction before you expand your niche.

Second, we start to flesh that person out
- Are they male or female?
- Young or old?
- Where do they live?
- What job do they do?

It's good to have some demographic knowledge of who that person is, but it doesn't stop there.

Third, we dig into the psychographics of that person
- What are their values?
- Their hopes?
- Their dreams?
- Their fears?
- Their beliefs?

Essentially, how do they experience the world and what beliefs do they have that are relevant to your business?

Lastly... we put it all together

You need to flesh that person out so that they feel like a living, breathing human that you could sit down and have a chat with.

Once you get to that stage, marketing your business and generating leads is made so. much. *easier*.

You no longer feel like you're standing in the middle of Oxford Street, straining to make your voice heard. Instead, you can be the equivalent of Tesco using their intercom at 5 pm on Valentine's Day to tell all of the last-minute shoppers about the 2-for-1 sale on red roses in Aisle 4.

Right message, to the right audience, at the right time –

that's the aim.

I've built multiple businesses to seven figures with one consistent thought process and method of marketing that works repeatedly, no matter the industry or niche.

Building a business is hard, let's get that out of the way. There are ups and downs, one step back for every two steps forward, sometimes you may wonder why you even started a business. Don't worry, a lot of business owners and entrepreneurs have had the same thought many times.

You'll forever live with the entrepreneur's curse; when you're working you feel you should be with your family and when you are with your family, you feel guilty for not working. Many an entrepreneur and business owner has thought about getting a "real job" or have even regretted starting their business.

This is because of one important missing piece of the puzzle.

No one teaches you how to be a business owner and no one teaches you how to *market* effectively and efficiently to *attract* your ideal client.

On the journey to building a successful business (whatever that means to you), many of the problems you face are linked to poor or a lack of marketing in some way:

- Not enough sales = marketing
- Not enough profit = marketing
- Not enough time = marketing
- Unable to scale = marketing

You may be thinking, hang on, how can "not enough time" be linked to marketing? In my experience of building a business in an ineffective way for almost ten years (and still having success), when you lack time, it's because you haven't attracted enough ideal clients that support the right profits, which means you haven't built the team to give you time.

But just imagine for a moment your perfect client arriving at your door (or on the phone or via your website) five times a day, five days a week, 52 weeks a year.

That is what I want for you.

We live in a digital era. You cannot escape social media and the online world, which means the opportunity to use all the free platforms, build an organic following, and attract leads and clients has never been greater.

No matter the industry you work in, the methods in this book apply to you. I started using them to generate seven figures in the mortgage industry and I now use the exact same methods to build other businesses in the education, coaching, health and mentoring space.

The methods I share in this book to attract your ideal client, get their attention, and double your sales are the exact methods I have used and taught to 1000s of business owners to bring in high-quality leads at virtually no cost.

By the end of this book, I want you to know why now is the time to begin marketing yourself, to understand how you are the differentiator from the next "expert" in your industry, and how building your online personal brand and bringing your leads closer to you is going to double your sales.

When you control your marketing – by understanding the five steps in this book – you reduce your spend and bring in your ideal clients. The goal is not to appeal to all clients, the goal is to appeal to the ones you love and to make sure you are the first in line when they need your product or service.

I am going to show you how to create more leads, sales, profit, and time so you can earn more, work less, and live a lifestyle you love.

> **NOTE**
> This book will not include specifics on individual social media channels since that would make this book quickly outdated. There are constantly new channels available, algorithms are always changing, and my goal is to give you the marketing tactics and strategies that stand the test of time and work across any channel.
>
> You can use this book to understand marketing and then dive deeper into learning about a specific channel that applies to your niche or ideal client.

Who Am I?

In my first ten years of being self-employed (from 2006 to 2015), I built a hugely successful business, but not without sacrifice. I had to go back to work three days after my first daughter was born because I was spending £20,000 per month on buying life insurance leads, paying agencies, and using third-party companies and introducers to control my future.

I was trapped and the worry of not feeding the monsters that gobbled up my money and spat out low-quality leads made me miss so much. It made me build a business I hated and go to work feeling nervous, anxious, and, quite frankly, depressed. Can you relate to this?

So, what changed?

In 2015, after seven years of building a life insurance brokerage, I decided to move home. I approached my bank about a mortgage and was surprised when they said no because of the way I paid myself as a business owner.

Having been a mortgage broker from 2003 to 2009 (prior to the credit crunch, which caused my pivot to insurance), I set about finding a way to get approved. I spoke to 100s of lenders, which indirectly made me an early expert in self-employed and business owner mortgages. Finally, in October of 2015, we moved into our dream home, and I made the decision to downsize my insurance brokerage, keeping two of my 13-person team. I started all over again on January 1st, 2016, with new marketing, a fresh message, and using social media.

Since 2016, I have spent six figures on my personal and business development, the majority revolving around marketing and attracting my ideal client. I have taken insights and lessons from industries both in the UK and abroad, applied them to my businesses to attract my ideal client day in day out, and the results are ten times the ROI (return on investment) in sales.

In many industries (especially the FS industry in the UK) there are people who will always say "you cannot do that" or "social media doesn't work" and back in 2015, I would have agreed with them. I was so sick of seeing my friends' dinner pictures, hearing the "woe is me" stories looking for attention, cats riding on skateboards, and the constant negativity online, so I hardly used social media.

Then I saw a guy called Jamie Alderton use online videos to go from being made redundant from the army to setting up a gym studio, sharing his journey, and becoming a champion at standing on a stage in his pants.

I thought well, if he can do it, I can definitely do it in the mortgage industry. So, in January of 2016, I started posting online and by June 2016, I was *sort of* confident enough to do video.

I've heard ever excuse under the sun from my students for why they can't start making videos.

- I hate the sound of my voice…
- I don't have time…
- I've got to put make up on… (admittedly, not one I personally struggled with)
- What will my friends say…

I'll tell you now, your first posts will be shit, but you only get better by doing it, so stop making excuses.

By October, I did my first live video and in November 2016, I did 30 live videos on Facebook for 30 days. The worry I had about being on social media disappeared and by 2017, I had developed a passion for marketing; taking someone who doesn't know you yet and getting them to start a relationship with you, become a follower, and buy from you.

My businesses are built based on the methods I have used since 2016, and I continue to use and develop them because I *love* marketing, social media, and lead generation.

More so, I love doing things differently. I love hearing the old schoolers say it will never work and proving them wrong. I love seeing what works in other industries, niches, and disrupting the FS industry by continuing to improve and stand out from the norm.

My purpose and passion have grown and evolved, and I am truly living to my values knowing that I am helping you to earn more, work less and live your dream lifestyle, giving you more time to do what you love with who you love. Showing you how to market your business will help you build a reputation as an expert, educate your clients to make more informed decisions, and most importantly, give you a profitable and fun business.

No matter what industry you are in, no matter if you want to generate local, national, or international leads, the principles in this book will work for you.

If that's what you want, keep reading because I am going to show you how you can use those methods to build a brand, a business, and generate leads without using third-party companies or marketing agencies. When you take control of your marketing, you will have more leads, sales, profit, and time!

The PRO Mentality

P.R.O. = PERSEVERANCE leads to RESULTS, which creates OPPORTUNITY

When you become self-employed, no one teaches you how to be self-employed or a business owner.

You leave the safety and security of a job with a big vision, with a goal to have more time, with a plan to do things your way, and what happens is you soon lack and lose all those things you set out to achieve.

No doubt you have spent hours, possibly even years, learning your trade, getting better at your craft. But how much time have you spent learning business? Learning marketing? Or even sales?

This book is the beginning of your journey to understanding the basic principles of marketing, social media, and lead generation. If you put into action the methods outlined in this book, you will get results.

You'll develop the mindset to keep going when it gets hard, to do what you need to even when you don't want to. There are days I don't want to go live, when I have nothing to say, when I cannot think of a post to share – but I still do it for my audience, for my clients, and for you.

You won't become amazing overnight; it may take weeks, months, possibly even years, but do not compare yourself and your journey to others. You don't know what's going on behind the scenes.

A PRO commits. You put a stake in the ground, create a vision, devise a plan, and take the required action.

Warren Buffet says, *"the best investment you can make is in yourself, because it pays dividends for a lifetime."*

What I absolutely love about marketing is you understand how to put £1 in and get £2 back, even £5 or £10. You can try and figure it all out on your own by reading all the books and listening to podcasts, but a PRO understands time is money – they let go to grow, for example:

- Let go of tasks someone else can do – delegate the £10 tasks.
- Let go of ego – there is always something and someone to learn from.
- Let go of a negative mindset and surround yourself with the right people.

"I don't have time" is not an excuse. It's time to prioritise your learning, action, marketing, and sales. The methods in this book will continue to evolve as social media and the online world does, but the basic principles will never change.

Now is the time to become a PRO.

Basic Business & Marketing Principles

The first two jobs I had in sales were cold calling and door knocking. Cold calling for a local company in Essex called Zeneth Windows was fun; I'd ring 50 cold leads a day and get sworn at, the phone put down on me, occasionally someone nice who wanted to chat, and *very* occasionally, a sale.

It was the exact same with door knocking in my early career as a mortgage adviser. I'd pull up at someone's house to get a deal done and then spend the next hour or two hitting the street. Come rain or shine, I was there, trudging the road, handing out leaflets, asking questions, and meeting new clients.

In both jobs, I began to see the importance of knowing my numbers. I knew if I knocked ten doors, I would always get one YES and book an appointment for the next week.

Looking back, it helped to build up some resilience and a bit of a hard shell to negative feedback, which has most definitely helped with my social media marketing efforts and what I will cover in this book.

In my first job, my manager gave me some sound advice

that still applies today:

- Look for the no's because it brings you one step closer to your yes.
- Invest one to three hours *every day* in finding new business/lead generation.
- Get your paperwork right first time; it may take you longer but going back to sort it out when you have done another five deals is a nightmare.

I still stand by these principles today without fail. But now, the way I achieve number two is *very* different. The goal is less stress, to be more effective, and way more efficient. An important factor is volume; the more people you ring, the more doors you knock, the more first appointments you set, or simply, the more you post on a social media channel, the more results you get.

In marketing, you want to find the yes; a client who engages and submits their details or picks up the phone and gives you a call. However, there is so much information out there and so many other people vying for attention that it can be hard to get the quality of lead and enquiry we did years ago.

Telephone sales and door-knocking were one-to-one but today, the best leverage of time is one-to-many. Speaking in public (a massive fear I have overcome) and marketing online are all about one-to-many but even then, you are not looking to connect with everyone, you are looking for the ones who like you and who are your ideal client.

I'm going to talk more about it later in the book, but it's relevant now because this is how sales have changed. No longer is it about making a sale there and then, no longer can you get the conversions you used to by expecting everyone to do business with you NOW, and if you pitch to that small number of leads (as I did for ten years), you will always find your quality of lead is poor.

Marketing is the most important function of a business

Imagine for a moment you have the best idea, the best product, the absolute best service that everyone needs and should most definitely want.

- How do you make sales?
- How do you get it into people's hands?

Marketing. Without marketing your brand, product, or services, you do not have a business. If people don't know who you are, what you sell, or what you do, then you will never create sales or profit.

And yet, if marketing is the lifeblood of any business, why do so many business owners fail to learn it? Because it can be outsourced, it can be put into someone else's hands, and this is why so many people find business so hard.

As you begin to make sales, you *should* leverage your admin and finances to an expert, but that's another story and another book for another day.

WHEN YOU START OUT, YOU WEAR **THE FOUR KEY HATS** OF A BUSINESS OWNER:

1 MARKETING **2** SALES **3** ADMIN **4** FINANCES

Your job as a business owner is to step into the role of managing director (MD) who directs the workflow. No one understands your brand and business better than you, so it's going to be insanely hard to find someone as passionate about your business as you. Your goal is to focus more on the strategy and direction of the business along with the marketing.

You can recruit salespeople, you can teach salespeople, you can get admin and finances covered by someone else, but you cannot replace the passion and drive for your product or service. No one is going to be better at selling your company to clients than you.

There are parts of marketing you can leverage to others who are experts. You can have a social media persona, Google ads, Facebook ads, blog writing, web design, email marketing… the list goes on. But your job is to become a generalist in every area and drive the marketing strategy, allowing others to repurpose it and share it far and wide on your behalf.

The brand, message, and voice must come from you if

you really want to stand out and be an expert, and we will talk about your personal brand and business brand later in the book.

The bottom line is that if you want to have a fun and profitable lifestyle business, then you need to become better at marketing. The best business owners out there today—Grant Cardone, Gary V, Richard Branson—are the best marketers. They drive the brand and the market, and that puts them in the top 5%.

Building your pipeline

The internet has changed the marketing game by emphasising the importance of AIDA – a model that has been used for over 100 years. It's the perfect way to help your reader notice your content and take action.

AWARENESS

INTEREST

DESIRE

ACTION

As a salesperson, you spend your time looking for the

action takers, the ones who are ready to buy your product or service now. However, this makes up the smallest amount of opportunity, as you can see in the "action" part of the AIDA model.

In marketing, you must speak to clients who don't even know you yet, with the goal of making them *aware* of you. When you capture someone in the awareness phase, you build 'know, like, and trust', and they travel down the buying cycle with you in mind at every step. Eventually, they become a loyal fan who will only work with you.

I stumbled across this method after spending ten years doing no marketing. Little did I know that finding a niche, speaking to one type of client, and giving them valuable content that solved their problem would move clients through the buying cycle, turning them into action takers with only me in mind. This happened because I had caught them early, so they were not planning to use anyone else other than me. They saw me as the expert in my niche and over the years, I have used this simple method to build an audience and sell in multiple industries.

Here is a real-world experience of AIDA in action.

Awareness

Every night when I stop work, we sit down as a family and have dinner. We then move into the bath and bed phase with our children and eventually slump on to the sofa for 1-2 hours of Netflix (and chill if I'm lucky).

But our sofa had become old and over time I moved from, "the cushion is getting soft, we should think about a new sofa", to "my back hurts, we need a new sofa". The more uncomfortable it became, the more we became interested in finding a new one.

Interest

The decision was made, and we started searching online for options. We looked at different styles, colours, and sizes to figure out what we wanted next. After narrowing it down to a couple sofas, it was time to hit the shops for a look.

Desire

My wife had a few in mind in DFS and Sofology, so we went to both shops and checked them all out before coming home to look at Trustpilot reviews for the specific sofas.

Action

Eventually, we settled on one and went to the shop to make out final purchase. But most of our decision had been made before we even went to the shop to purchase.

No matter what you are buying, you'll follow the same process:

- **Awareness** – I need a holiday.
- **Interest** – Look at some holiday destinations, ask friends for advice, narrow down a country.
- **Desire** – Check out reviews, find out if anyone has been there before, get some prices, compare prices on a variety of websites.
- **Action** – Buy a holiday package.

If your ideal clients aren't aware of you early in this process, then it's highly unlikely they are going to take action with you.

> **NOTE**
> In social media marketing, if all your leads are only on your social media pages and not in your own database, they are not yours. Your goal is to take clients from free platforms in the awareness phase and move them into your database (i.e., the interested phase which you now own). Then you continue to build the relationship with them on social media and in your database.

Jeffrey Gitomer (American Author & sales Trainer) once said, "Clients don't like to be sold, but they love to buy." Raising client awareness, getting them interested in what you have to say, and building their desire for your product or services means they will only take action with you when they're ready.

Forget about selling; marketing is about networking, relationship building, connection, and solving problems for your ideal client. If you do this, you will never have to sell again, the action takers will come to you already sold.

We will revisit the AIDA model later in the book when we come to content marketing.

Buying leads is pointless

Ten years of buying names, numbers, and email addresses off the internet made me build a business I hated. I tried everything to get a client to buy from me, buying cold data and phoning 100 people to get one yes. Over the years, we even tried online survey data…

- Have you got life insurance? Yes?
- Would you like to reduce the amount you spend? No?
- Would you like a quote to protect your income, your family, or your mortgage?

It was really hard work. It required a telesales team to pass the enquiries onto a sales team and, worst of all, there was no client loyalty or understanding of our brand, the benefits of which we will talk about later in this book.

With internet-purchased leads, in particular, you need to be on them within five minutes of the enquiry or you risk losing the sale to someone else. Your pitch and process need to be slick to make the lead believe they don't need to speak to someone else. You need to win that business early and win the lead over to get the sales – it's cutthroat. This was my main method for ten years; everything was scripted, automated, systemised, managed, and monitored to within an inch of the salesperson's life.

If you want to be the Wolf of Wall Street—or in the film *Boiler Room*—feel free to build your business this way.

This model requires constant effort. You spend X to make Y and there are many variables outside of your control. For example, many lead providers are adamant they don't multi-sell, but it happens, and it's hard to prove.

Buying leads keeps you busy, but the quality can be insanely poor. You end up only speaking to 50% of what you purchase because the other half don't answer or are just invalid numbers. But by constantly ringing for 3-5 days, 3-5 times per day, you feel productive, even though you're being ineffective and inefficient with your time.

The amount of time my team used to waste calling low-quality leads was eye-watering. Yes, we made a decent profit, but I was stressed, worried, and anxious. If I stopped paying £20,000 a month, then the business was going under not long after. I had to keep investing in leads to make more money but there was never consistency in the quality of leads.

I could bang on about my mistakes all day but let me finish here by saying building your business by buying leads is setting yourself up to fail. Not learning the methods in this book is setting yourself up to fail. To build a truly profitable business, you *need* to take control of your marketing.

Stop solely relying on introducers, partnerships, and recommendations

Relying solely on introducers and partnerships to give you leads (like an estate agent supplying a mortgage broker) puts you under their spell. They hold all the cards, you have to be at their beck and call, you work on their terms, and you may have to pay them a percentage of the sale for the privilege.

The other problem with introducers is having no control over the quality of the enquiry. What if they choose to use someone else, or worse still, their business closes? Relying on another business for your leads is a risk and can be unpredictable.

Another unpredictable method is using referrals and recommendations. I see many business owners who wear *"I get all my leads from referrals"* like a badge of honour.

While it's important to get recommendations, it's very unpredictable and stressful not knowing where your next lead and sale is coming from.

You cannot build a fun and profitable lifestyle business by relying on someone else or without having a predictable way of attracting your ideal client. The methods in this book will show you how to take control of your marketing and make your marketing predictable.

Social media marketing is just like networking

The only real difference is it's virtual and online. When you network face-to-face, you must keep showing up week in week out before you begin to get massive results. You turn up to a networking meeting, you sit in a room with the same old faces once a month, you share ideas, you chat about everything except business (depending on the meeting you go to, not all are alike) in the hope that one day someone will recommend you to a friend or someone they know to generate business. Occasionally, when you have been going long enough, you build a partnership with someone that refers you a lot of business and you begin to get a lot of leads.

Or there is one large networking group with big upfront fees, and you are put under pressure to bring other members in and make regular referrals. If you are someone who needs huge pressure and accountability, this may work well for you. But if you are like me and like accountability without the pressure then avoid those and keep reading.

Now, it may seem like I have just slagged of networking, but I haven't, it can most definitely work *when used effectively* and when you play the long game. And it's the same with social media. I believe in multiple streams of leads and networking, and it can work and will work providing you do it correctly. But anyone who tells you it works has put in the hours, the hard work, they have befriended a lot of leads, and, over time, they have become known in their niche and people refer them because of it.

But remember, it can be unpredictable.

What hasn't worked for me is the low-cost monthly networking. I tried several for a few months and never had great results from it. It was like people wanted to be friends instead of growing their businesses and taking things to the next level. I also never really learned anything, which is one of my highest values; I love to learn, implement, and grow, and that just didn't happen. The hours I invested could have been much better spent.

My personal method of networking is higher ticket. I pay for a course to solve a specific problem, to learn, and be with a room full of like-minded people. Sometimes that could be £300 for one day, others could be £5,000 for five days, but my goal is to connect with people like me. Because networking—just like social media marketing—is not about trying to find and appeal to everyone.

Remember, people like you, will like you.

Social media marketing and networking are not about *everyone,* they are about the few you can help, that you like, and who like you. Your friends are your friends because of the things you have in common *not* because of the product and service you provide.

The problem with a networking meeting, and where you may go wrong, is ending up spending time with the five people out of 30 you really get on with. It's natural to want to be with people you have things in common with, but this limits your opportunity.

Social media and online marketing give you the opportunity to reach more people and find more people just like you much more easily than networking. Sometimes it can happen overnight; many of my mentees have put out a post or video online and found they get leads for their business within hours (because they follow a simple method that works).

I remember one client telling me, "My friends messaged me and didn't even realise that's what I did for a job." Now that's insane, but it also shows the power of social media. When people know what you do, you have more chance of getting leads, clients, and sales, providing people *like* you.

As your audience grows and new people come into your world, you have the opportunity to meet new people and bring new people into your network, which gives you the chance to get more leads, clients, and sales.

With networking events, the more you go, the more people remember who you are and the more leads, clients, and sales you get. If you play the long game with social media and consistently put yourself out there online, you are networking. You are building relationships, people begin to know, like, and trust you. The weird thing is your "friends" or followers will begin recommending you even if they haven't used your product or service because you become known for who you are and what you do.

So, how do you accomplish this online? When it comes to social media marketing, the overall goal is to build a personal and business brand that people trust.

Notes

The Lead Generation Method

When it comes to marketing and generating leads, there is a simple five-stage process you can follow. The journey you are going to embark upon in this book is as follows:

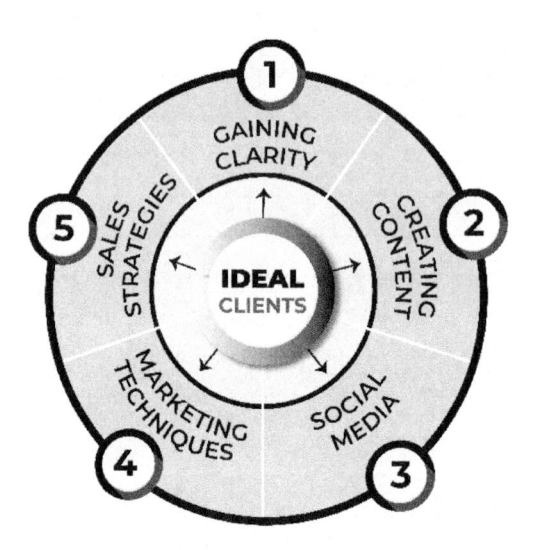

1. Gaining Clarity
2. Creating Content
3. Social Media
4. Marketing Techniques
5. Sales Strategies

(Ideal Clients at the center)

I could write a whole book on sales alone and maybe I will one day, but this book will focus on lead generation. Of course, I can't end it without giving you some knowledge and skills to turn those new leads into paying clients, which is why we'll end on step five – sales.

If you take action on everything from here on in, I guarantee that you will be able to generate more leads, increase your sales, and earn more while working less.

STEP 1
Gaining Clarity

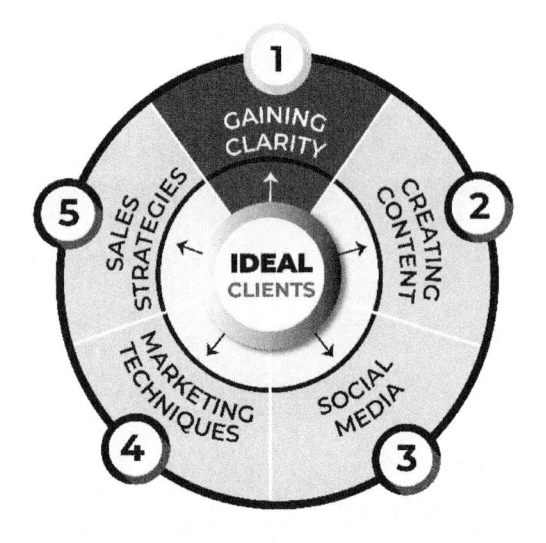

Finding a niche

People "go self-employed" for a number of advertised benefits: more money, more freedom, more control, etc., and most self-employed people will shout, *"It's the best thing I ever did!"*

But I've seen it with my own eyes. The majority of self-employed people and business owners, especially advisers, do *not* live that lifestyle. Most work longer hours, have more stress, and greater responsibility on their shoulders. And there's less certainty about the next six months than someone who is employed. If they do go for the laid-back approach and work fewer hours, their take-home income takes a *massive* hit.

The sad thing is that it really doesn't have to be this way. The dream you were sold of higher income, more freedom, and more control *is* totally possible. With some tweaks to how you operate, you can double your income with half the effort that you're putting in now.

And achieving that ultimately boils down to one thing: **thinking like a real business owner instead of a hustler.**

A hustler is reactive and owned by their "business", so makes short-term decisions. But a business owner is in control and makes proactive, strategic, long-term decisions.

The first thing that a business owner needs to take control of is the way they bring new clients into the business. If you buy names and numbers, rely on introducers, or have a single source of leads, *you're not in control.*

That's why I'm a huge advocate of generating your own clients with online marketing. Once you do, you'll see a snowball effect.

- You generate clients that you love to work with.
- You put systems and processes in place to save time.
- You work to increase your sales, so you need fewer clients and save even more time.

That puts you on an accelerated path to clearing

£10,000, £20,000, £50,000+ per month while working a normal work week.

Imagine how big an impact that will have on the rest of your life. Because that's why we do this, right? So, we can do what we love, with who we love?

Investing your time and energy into taking back control and chasing that self-employed dream will be the best thing you ever did.

Who do you serve?

Clarity is so important; it is the foundation of my coaching and mentoring and it should be the foundation of your marketing. If you don't know who you are or who you best serve, how can you possibly gain their attention?

This step is often overlooked or done half-hearted and so the results are equally mediocre. You need to start a marketing plan by getting real clarity on your ideal client, and you do that by first gaining a deeper understanding of your personal brand.

Once you are clear on who you are, you focus on your client in the same way, while also being aware of where they are in their journey vs. where they want to be. Once we know that, you can build and market a business that solves those problems and helps clients avoid the mistakes they don't know they are going to make.

> **NOTE**
> Prolific beats perfect. As you work through the upcoming chapters, if you constantly seek perfection in your marketing, you won't be able to test, review, tweak, and repeat. Creating content gives clarity, and with every piece of content, you move closer to more leads.

- Your first blog will be rubbish.
- Your first video will be rubbish.
- Your first style and branding will be rubbish.

When you accept that and understand that imperfect practice makes progress, you can just create and get your message, content, and marketing out into the world for people to see. Your biggest fans will want to go on that journey with you, so start producing and creating *now*.

> **NOTE**
> *Everything we are about to talk about is content.*

Finding your niche or demographic

Focus is key to getting results with your personal brand. You can fast-track results by owning a niche or clearly understanding your demographic.

Who is that ideal client you love to deal with five days a week, 52 weeks a year? Your goal is to attract that client to your business, to pre-sell them on the idea that you are their solution.

We will talk about how in the next section, but for now, think about whether you want to own a niche or focus on a specific demographic instead.

Remember, your target audience is *not* everyone. Your task in defining your target group is to **identify and understand your client so you can own that space.**

Niche marketing

Niche marketing is a strategy that focuses on a unique target market. Instead of marketing to everyone who could benefit from a product or service, you focus exclusively on one group. A niche generally:

- Has less competition
- Solves a particular problem
- Has a huge amount of satisfaction for you
- Has a higher chance of customer retention

The most effective and efficient niches are job title, industry, or occupation. Other niches are a specific problem, product or service, or even a location.

It's powerful when you can say...
"I only deal with _____."

The benefit of niche marketing is that it allows you to differentiate yourself, become the authority, and resonate more deeply with a distinct client. Rather than be like everyone else who offers the same type of product or service, niche marketing helps you stand out, appear more valuable, and build a stronger, longer-lasting connection with your ideal audience.

This allows you to target one sector or industry and repurpose content with different titles that attract specific micro-niches. A micro-niche is a smaller niche inside a niche (e.g., self-employed is a niche, limited company business owners or sole traders are a micro-niche).

To find the right niche, you need to start with something or someone you love, identify the problems and needs of that ideal client, and carry out market research to define the profitability.

Demographic marketing

Demographic marketing is very similar to niche marketing. The main difference is your ideal client is narrowed down by demographic factors such as age, gender, or income.

Your target market should be based on audience research or client data, not a gut feeling. You need to be willing to learn as you go, adapt, and go after the people who really want to buy from you, even if they're not the clients you originally set out to reach.

I love the UK supermarket analogy:

- Aldi or Lidl
- Tesco
- Sainsbury
- M&S or Waitrose

I'm sure you will agree they all have a demographic they work with, and they know who they best serve. Occasionally, a consistent Tesco shopper might fancy some "luxury" and pop to M&S or Waitrose. But each brand knows who they are targeting and the message they use appeals to that shopper and the price point of the products matches the demographic.

This is the same way you should look at speaking to your client. How you talk to a 20-year-old will differ from how you talk to a 60-year-old. The language used will be totally different. So, when thinking about either a niche or a demographic, you need to consider:

- Age
- Gender
- Marital status
- Hobbies
- Interests

You need to get inside your ideal client's head because the clearer you understand who they are now, the problems they have, mistakes they make, and the challenges they need to overcome, the more you will get results from your marketing.

Your ideal client is someone who likes you, loves your social media, buys everything you sell, is willing to promote you to others, and sees the real value in your product or services.

Knowing who you love to work with makes telling your story so much easier because you can speak to your client in a way that motivates them to act, so get to know them better than they know themselves.

Mistakes lead to problems

When it comes to understanding your clients, you need to know the most common mistakes they make that lead to the problems they have. This gives you a two-pronged attack in your marketing and it enables you to speak to your clients at different stages.

Remember AIDA earlier in the book? By talking about your clients' mistakes when they are in the attention phase, you are highlighting what they could do wrong and the problems it will lead to, so you *should* become a logical choice for solutions.

When highlighting a problem, your client may have also already made the mistake; they are seeing, hearing, or feeling it there and then. They are most likely in the interest and desire phase, and they need that problem solved.

I am a huge fan of marketing to your client at the earliest point of buying. In my mortgage business, I had to ask myself, what is the first thought clients have about moving? How can I position finance as the first thing they think about?

I realised when my bank said no to my mortgage application in 2015, the mistake I made was leaving it until the last minute, getting my accounts and books done, then going to the bank. Had I known the criteria long before I applied, I could have set goals and targets in my business which would have set me up for success, based on the lender. Instead, I found the house I wanted first and was under pressure throughout the process. It's why I wrote my Amazon bestseller, *The Self-Employed Mortgage Guide*, which talks about the mistakes I made, the problems they caused, and helps clients to overcome them.

Think about problems and mistakes your clients make because it will be a core part of your marketing to attract clients to you.

When I was working on the marketing for my mortgage business, I found a recurring mistake my clients were making was self-assessing their own tax returns. An accountant can easily save you more in tax than the time and investment in their services, so it was an easy solution I could provide my clients to show I was an expert in my niche.

Avoiding the mistakes in your marketing

You are no doubt making mistakes that are causing you problems when attracting your ideal client. To benchmark your current lead generation performance and identify opportunities for attracting your ideal client and increasing your sales, you can use my free marketing analyser. It'll generate a marketing score and show you exactly where you need to improve:

https://scorecard.theleadgenerationguide.co.uk

Building your brands

There's a trend gripping many industries, especially the financial services industry and it's **VITAL** that you jump on board.

Got your attention? Good, because it's important that you hear this.

I've been using social media to market my business since 2016, and it's fair to say that the decision to grow my brand on social media changed my life. When I started, I saw an opportunity based on what people were doing in other industries but in hindsight, it was the financial service's slow acceptance of this trend that gave me a head start.

Now, we've reached the tipping point. A social presence for self-employed people and advisers is a key part of generating business, and as per Forbes a study from November 2020 pinpointed a few things that add weight to this. They found that a recommendation from friends influences the buying decision of 81% of people, and that definition of 'friend' in the social media age is very loose. You can build a friendship with a friend request, a few post likes, and a comment.

The same survey discovered that a social media post by a company influences 78% of people, and these numbers are only going to increase over time. Every year, more of the 'old-school' leave the mortgage space and are replaced by 'social-savvy' Millennials and Gen Z who demand social engagement.

It has been a frustration of mine that this trend has screamed in our faces, but advisers are still so slow to react. And it has not been for want of trying for many people online. Posting as little as once per day on one social media channel can have a huge impact on building your business and generating leads.

One question that always comes up is whether you should build your personal brand or business brand. Which is most important?

Business brand

A business brand is about your corporate vision, mission, and values. This is what will make your company and business stand out from others. It also helps you to build a culture and team environment that people want to be part of.

Your business brand is the promise you make to your clients about what they can expect and what they will get. It's about feeling and emotion, more than a logo, design, or swag.

Your business has its own name, giving it the power to be bigger than you. You can have a team and you can go global. If you choose to name your business after your own name, there are limitations to your level of growth. Generally, a business brand with a family name is more localised and stands out in a local area, rather than on an international level.

Personal brand

A personal brand is about the person, the leader of the business, the owner or entrepreneur. It's what people say about you when you're not in the room. It's being clear about what you stand for and what you stand against.

In the online world of networking or building relationships, people buy from people. If you want your business brand to grow ten times faster, you need to build your personal brand alongside your business image. Here are a few examples:

- **Richard Branson: 4.8 million Instagram followers**
- **Virgin: 234K (Oct 2022)**

From a business brand perspective, you know what you are going to get from Virgin because you see Richard Branson's personal brand. The two brands are not just aligned, they are extremely similar. Clients will use Virgin purely because they like Richard, and your leads and clients will feel the same about you.

- **The Rock (Dwayne Johnson): 342 million Instagram followers**
- **Under Armour: 8.3 million (Oct 2022)**

Business brands want to align with personal brands that share the same values and leverage their audience to promote their products. Under Armour released a "#ProjectRock" range knowing that his audience would lap up trainers, earphones, sweat tops, and more in minutes. The speed at which these products sold out is insane.

- **Jessica Alba: 19.9 million Instagram followers**
- **Honest: 1 million (Oct 2022)**

The company began in 2008 when a pregnant Jessica Alba couldn't find reasonably priced natural and eco-friendly baby products and had the idea for a "clean and natural" products brand. Leveraging her personal brand, she has sold dozens of products, including fashionable diapers for babies, detergents, and wipes. In 2021, the IPO valued Honest at $1.44 billion.

> **NOTE**
> A key part of business is relationships and the best way to build and attract new relationships is to have a personal brand that businesses know is aligned with theirs.
>
> I am a massive fan of lifestyle businesses. To me, that's about building a business that allows me to do more of what I love with who I love. As a lifestyle business owner, the differentiator that can make your business stand out from the crowd—and be chosen over a huge, faceless corporate brand—is YOU.

One of my very first students in 2019 took my advice and niched in "CIS Mortgages" (Construction Industry Scheme, generally self-employed trades people). He went all in; website, social media channels, content, design, even wearing a hard hat in his videos to stand out in the feed to his ideal client.

People travel from all over the UK to work with David Sharpstone and pay him more than they will pay any other mortgage broker because of his strong niche. They see him as the solution to their problem and know that he understands their problems and mistakes better than anyone else. He has doubled down on his niche and owns that specific space in the minds of his customers.

He estimates that this one simple decision has made him an additional six figures consistently each year.

The power of personal brand

People buy from people and people like you will like you, so the more clarity you have over your personal brand from a personal development point of view, the more you will resonate with people and stand out from the noise. The goal is not to be liked by everyone, your goal is to find those like you or those who share your common goals and interests.

The core questions to ask yourself are:

- What do you stand for?
- What do you stand against?
- What do you love?
- What do you hate?
- What do you want to be known for?

What you stand for will change over time as you develop and grow. The person I was in 2015 before discovering personal and business development was very different to the person I became by 2019. My personal brand evolved, as will you and yours.

Prolific beats perfect. It's both necessary and helpful to stand out, so embrace who you are and nail down the key message you want to focus on from day one.

When I started my business again in 2016, my key message was "helping self-employed people to get a mortgage".

As I created content, understood my clients more deeply, and got more results it became, "helping self-employed business owners and investors to buy and invest in property".

In 2019, with my Active team growing and my industry asking for lead generation help, I launched my coaching business with, "I help mortgage brokers generate leads and build their brokerages".

By 2021, having worked with more than 500 business owners, my focus became "I help advisers and business owners to increase their income without the stress of figuring it all out on their own to achieve a fun & profitable lifestyle business."

As you begin to create content, your vision, purpose, passion, and business will pivot, as will your message, but the one constant is going to be *you* throughout.

It's important to stay on brand; be authentic and genuine on a daily basis. No doubt you are an expert in your area and have a good reputation, which is why people use your product or services. It helps to share the real you—as your friends and family see you—with your clients, team, and social media because that is most authentic.

It's that authenticity that enables you to share your values. In my business, I don't just talk about mortgages, mentoring, and coaching; there are many aspects that link in, such as family and fitness, along with sharing the ups and downs in all those areas.

Sharing the ups and downs is taking clients on a journey with you. It's why movies are so great – because of the hero's journey. Just look at any Rocky film; we all know he is going to win in the end but losing and coming back to take the title is why those films are classics. You are living your own story, on your own rollercoaster, and showing that personal (and business) journey is what clients, especially fans, want to see.

Consistency is key
That goes for all social media channels. Your clients want to see you talking about your product or services and what's most important to you in life, and they want to see it for a long period of time. Your personal brand is not some get-rich-quick scheme, so don't treat it like one.

You should live your brand and make sure it's congruent with you. 'Active' is my company brand and when I set up my business in 2006, I spoke to my dad about names. His company was called Active Products and when we spoke about it, by its own definition, it was everything I embodied as a person.

Energetic, sporty, vigorous, dynamic, sprightly, involved, on the go, in action, powerful, effective.

It became my anchor, a constant reminder of how I should be, how my clients should perceive me, and the service they can expect from Active.

My coaching and mentoring business, PRO, also has a deeper meaning. It's not just being professional, "perseverance leads to results which creates opportunity" is the statement I live by. "Now is the time to become PRO" is my ethos and want for you after reading this book – to take action and be active now.

It could take six months, or it could take three years of consistency to see exceptional results. But if you want to build a strong brand, you need to focus, tell your story, stand out from the crowd, be consistent with your message, and be consistent with your output to see real results.

Leverage your personal brand
You don't need millions of followers or fans online, you only need a few who buy everything that you sell. You need to find that 20% of clients who want to be in your world, who are just like you, and they will make up 80% of your income and your results online.

1000 awesome fans spending £1,000 with you = £1 million.

Business really doesn't have to be complicated. Why spend all your life trying to make time for your family, working in a job you hate, when you can be passionate about something online, build an audience of clients who like you (locally, nationally, or internationally), and will buy from you over and over again?

If I can inspire you with one message reading this book it's this: strategic marketing will solve most of the problems in your business. There are hundreds of options when it comes to building your business; methods I will share later in this book that you can use to generate leads for your business. But when it comes down to it, all you need to do is find your awesome fans and they will give you the life you want.

Lack of leads, sales, profit, and time can be solved by better marketing and mastering only a few strategies, reinvesting the profit you make to leverage others, and building a brand to yield a lifetime of results.

Vanilla or marmite?

Your size of following not only depends on your marketing efforts, it depends on *you*. A decision you will have to make at some stage is how much of yourself you want to put out into the world. We all live in a comfort zone, and we all have the need to be loved or liked. It's a hard pill to swallow that not everyone likes us, and it can be even harder if someone trolls your content online or leaves a bad review.

The main thing to remember is most clients like vanilla. How can they not? It's plain and goes with everything. But marmite, love it or hate it, that is what creates a deeper connection and that is what divides opinion.

BMW or Audi? Football or Rugby? Loving one doesn't mean you don't like people in the other camp, but it does mean you create a preference, you create a deeper connection, and a more loyal following.

Generally, controversial or strong views are what divide opinion on your personal brand. Your client either chooses to agree or disagree and one statement could lose you the business. But it also builds a much more loyal following among clients who do like you.

Don't be vanilla. Which leaves the question, how much like marmite do you want to be?

Building a business brand

The key to building a successful business brand is not just colours, logo, and swag; you need a deeper thought process behind it. These visual aspects should actually be last on your list.

In the same way you thought about who you are as a personal brand, you should think about who and what your business represents as a company brand; how are you different? What do you stand for and stand against?

You want to build a business that has a deeper meaning, one that your clients and team can believe in, and which has a message you can take through your entire marketing plan.

Let me introduce, Vision, Mission, and Values. These will give you a purpose and a reason to run your business, they will attract a dedicated team and clients will want to work with you.

I have set out some examples below but remember, as you grow, develop, and build your business, these will change and evolve, as will everything in your marketing.

Vision: WHY you do what you do

A company vision is a road map setting out what you want the business to become and the big goal you want to achieve. Your company vision will undergo a lot of revisions during the early life of your business – remember, creating content brings clarity.

- Nike's vision: *To bring inspiration and innovation to every athlete in the world and if you have a body, you are an athlete.*

Mission: WHAT you do

A mission statement is what you do to achieve your vision. By focusing on your mission, you move closer to your vision with marginal gains. This is what your clients can expect to experience when working with your business.

> **NOTE**
> To break your mission down, you can include an annual or quarterly strategy which breaks down further into monthly and weekly actions.

- Nike's mission: *To do everything possible to expand human potential.*

How powerful is that?

Values: The identity behind the brand
These are the guiding principles that define success (three to four work best). Having values controls your every decision when actioning your mission. They act as a statement to the client in terms of what they can expect from you. Here are some examples:

- Integrity
- Boldness
- Honesty
- Trust
- Accountability
- Commitment to clients
- Passion
- Fun

You could have internal and external values – ones for your team and ones for your clients.

- Nike's values: *Inspiration, Innovation & Social Community Impact*

When it comes to recruitment, make sure your team are on board with your vision, mission and values.

I recommend you read *Start with Why* by Simon Sinek, in which he says, *"People don't buy what you do; they buy why you do it."* Your clients will buy into your brand, which makes it easier to attract them to you.

- What is it your clients are really buying?
- What is it they really want?
- And most importantly, why do they want it?

Your brand should answer these questions.

When someone is buying a home, is it the home they want or the feeling of safety, security, and an opportunity to create memories in that home that last a lifetime?

Think about the reason why clients buy and then ask why again and why again until you come to the root cause or feeling they want. If you can pinpoint your client's emotion and build that into your brand-led marketing, it will have a significant impact on your results.

Think about the last big purchase you made. When you are faced with endless choices through social media or recommendations, how do make your decisions? What influences you to select one brand over another. Take buying a car, for example, they all have the same basic function of getting us from A to Z?

The simple answer is emotion.

A great visual brand alone isn't enough. Your ideal clients have problems and make mistakes, and by highlighting them you begin to speak to their emotions, giving you the opportunity to present you and your business as the solution.

Evolving your solutions over time will give you clarity and focus and strengthen your marketing message. The outcome of this is far more trust and awareness, which reduces the friction of buying your products or services.

Step 1 Actions

1. What or who is your niche?
2. Write down your ideal client's 30 common mistakes.
3. Answer the core personal brand questions.
4. Define your company brand vision, mission, and values.

Notes

STEP 2
Creating Content

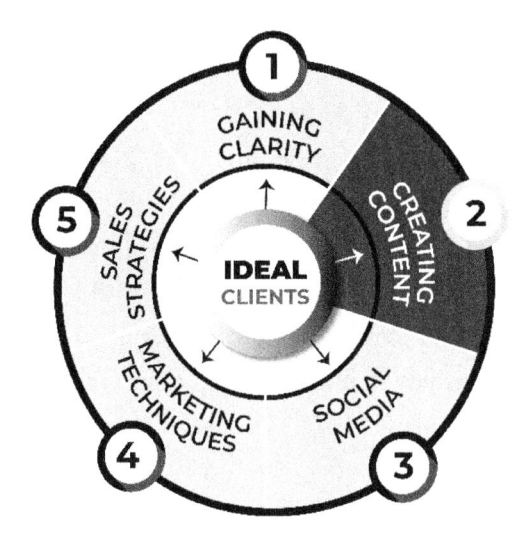

I want you to get into your car and drive to a village on the other side of the country beginning with the letter P.

Go!

If you start driving now, you may eventually find it a few years from now through trial and error after taking a *lot* of wrong turns. That's if you don't break down and give up.

Ok, this clearly isn't going to work. So, let's try again.

I want you to drive to a town called Pucklechurch, South Gloucestershire, the postcode is BS16.

Now it becomes a *lot* easier! Enter the destination into your Sat Nav and you can take the simplest and most direct route there.

It's the exact same concept with your business. If you don't know in crystal clear detail what your destination is, *how are you going to get there as fast as possible?*

Unfortunately, most people have a vague idea of what success looks like to them. So, they battle away, day-to-day, driven by gut instinct in a vague direction towards a 'goal'. They get pulled around in 100 different directions and never really get anywhere.

But once they get clear on what it is they're trying to achieve, the game changes.

You'll get clarity over what you need to do every day to move you in the direction of your goal. And if something doesn't move you closer to your goal, you know to cut it out. Best of all, you can reverse engineer the numbers of your vision and set KPIs (Key Performance Indicators) that help you track your progress.

This is the same with your content. If your content doesn't start with the end in mind, then you could be wasting a huge amount of energy.

With clarity around the problems and mistakes your ideal lead, client, or prospect is facing, we can use that information to create content. Everything we have discussed in the previous sections is content for your ideal client. Remember, people buy people and people like you will like you.

So, the question is, how do we use that information to gain their attention?

We live in an information and attention age; Google and YouTube have information so accessible to the world and the likes of social media—which we will chat about later—have got a lot of people online gunning for your attention. That is why personal brand is so important because the only difference in marketing is *you*.

You and I could do the same video, with the same content, for the same length of time, and we would appeal to different people. Yes, some may like us both, some may even hate us both (that's fine, they were never going to buy from us anyway), but some will prefer you and some will prefer me.

Look at the online fitness industry – there are so many styles of training, a million different diets, and everyone saying theirs is the best. There is a huge amount of information online which seemingly contradicts itself and there are 1000s of personal trainers doing videos, training routines, websites, plans, Instagram posts, etc.

How can you be expected to know right from wrong, what is good for you vs. good for everyone?

You don't have to. You can pick the PT who you believe can help you achieve the results you want, who talks the most amount of sense, and resonates the most with you.

The goal of your content marketing is to gain the attention of those that want to do business with you.

What is content marketing?

Content marketing is about producing valuable, relatable, relevant, and consistent content through a variety of channels and mediums to gain the attention of and retain clients. The ultimate goal is to build an audience of fans to build a more profitable business.

Marketing is impossible without great content, and everything we'll cover in the upcoming sections is free (better known as organic marketing), consisting of:

- Videos
- Podcasts
- Blogs
- Articles
- Social media posts
- PR
- And more

Instead of pitching your products or services all day every day, you give valuable and useful content to your ideal clients to help them solve their problems and mistakes, which, in turn, earns you the right to pitch your products and services.

Where so many business owners go wrong—and the issue with paid advertising as a sole method of marketing—is all you are doing is pitching to warm buyers. Content marketing is about networking and nurturing relationships to build a business for the future and one that is going to be sustainable over the long term.

When you take control of your content marketing, your message is much clearer and your clients are willing to pay you more than the next person, which leads to a more profitable business.

You can use content marketing to:

- Grow a Facebook group
- Fill spots on webinars
- Launch a book or podcast
- Fill an event
- Book speaking gigs
- Get more enquiries
- Boost social media engagement
- And more

For your brand to stand out from everyone else's, your content should always originate from you. No one knows your business better than you, no one will ever love it as much as you and, therefore, to have a clear message, you need to be the originator of the content. You can then use others to do the marketing (i.e., sharing it far and wide to 100s, 1000s, or even millions of people).

Quantity and quality are important in your content marketing efforts. You need to be posting enough to be seen and making sure that a good percentage of your content captures your clients' attention.

Too often I hear "social media doesn't work" or "no one is liking my content" and these problems come back to a quantity/quality issue. Your quantity will differ from my quantity; what might work for me might not work for you.

Engagement is one of the key factors to consider when content marketing. It's not about just posting and hoping it works, it's about consistently getting better at it.

My goal is to get better at making content, to have a clearer understanding of my client, and then focus on gaining their attention through quality and consistent content. My team's job is to market and share that content and be consistent with our plan.

Every week and month, the team and I review our content marketing based on our goal – the client, the problem we are solving, and the action we want them to take.

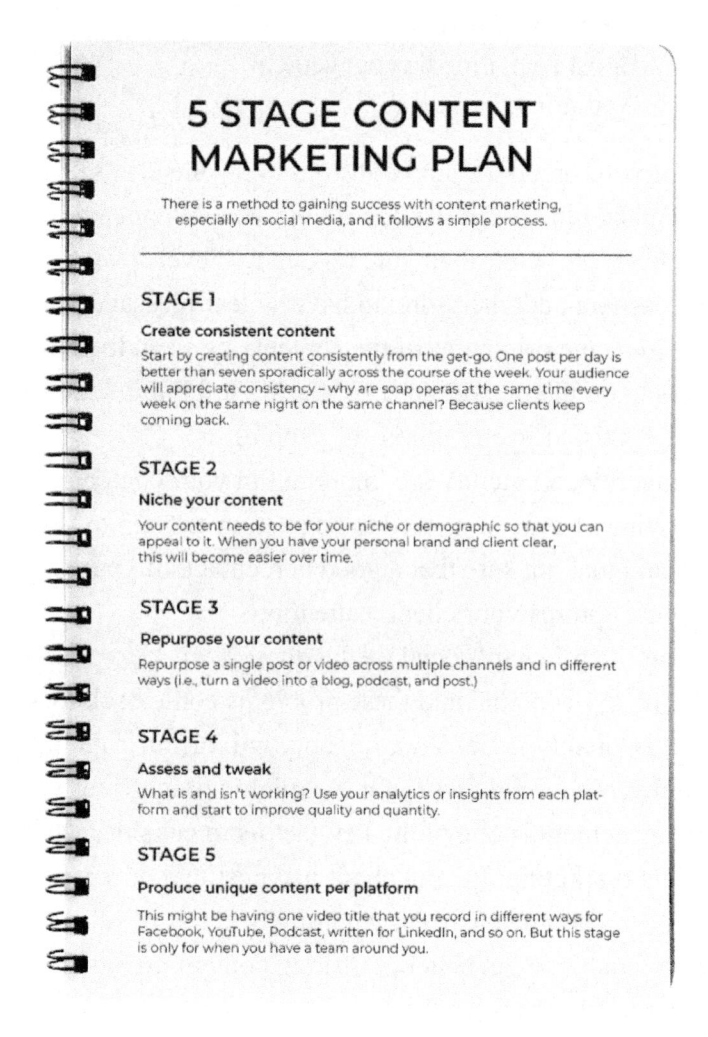

5 STAGE CONTENT MARKETING PLAN

There is a method to gaining success with content marketing, especially on social media, and it follows a simple process.

STAGE 1
Create consistent content

Start by creating content consistently from the get-go. One post per day is better than seven sporadically across the course of the week. Your audience will appreciate consistency – why are soap operas at the same time every week on the same night on the same channel? Because clients keep coming back.

STAGE 2
Niche your content

Your content needs to be for your niche or demographic so that you can appeal to it. When you have your personal brand and client clear, this will become easier over time.

STAGE 3
Repurpose your content

Repurpose a single post or video across multiple channels and in different ways (i.e., turn a video into a blog, podcast, and post.)

STAGE 4
Assess and tweak

What is and isn't working? Use your analytics or insights from each platform and start to improve quality and quantity.

STAGE 5
Produce unique content per platform

This might be having one video title that you record in different ways for Facebook, YouTube, Podcast, written for LinkedIn, and so on. But this stage is only for when you have a team around you.

I started stage five when I had a total team of six (plus myself). But that was a marketing journey that took from January 2016 to June 2021. My marketing team, at that time, had six members: social media video manager, copywriter, Instagram specialist, website developer, paid ads specialist, and a design expert.

No matter where you are in your journey, if you love content marketing as much as I do, it can happen a lot quicker, but it could also take you a hell of a lot longer. It depends on the quality of your content, your niche, and so many other components.

I have spent six figures learning how to be the most efficient and effective with some of the best mentors and trainers out there. The point is, every year it gets harder to stand out, get results, and make content marketing work for you because competition increases, channels change, and social media evolves.

If you have taken anything from this book so far, I hope you realise that now is the time to become PRO at creating content for your ideal client.

How to structure content

As mentioned earlier in the book, the AIDA format has been around for 100s of years, and it is still the simplest method for writing or recording your content.

AWARENESS — INTEREST — DESIRE — ACTION

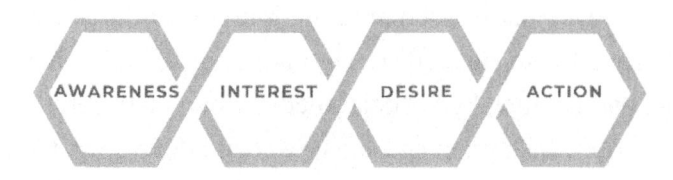

The AIDA model can be used to create a consistent flow of content. Whether that's video, written, podcast or blog, it is a method of turning someone who doesn't know you into someone who buys from you.

Awareness
Your headline is what will stop them scrolling and make them take notice of you. Make sure you use the information from your previous customers.

"If you are…" or "As a…" are both great ways to start your headline.

Interest
You have their attention, now you need to keep their interest. Here are some ways you can do this:

- Explain how their problem is negatively impacting them.
- Give them information that corrects a misconception they have.
- Tell a story about a client that faced a similar issue.
- Educate and inform the viewer.

Desire
Here, you move past the interest stage, and try to elicit

some emotion in the reader. You want to build their desire to take the next step. Ways to do this are:

- Show them there is light at the tunnel and a solution to their problem.
- Tell them the benefits of working with you and the results others have got.
- Add some urgency and a reason why they need to act now.

Action

Now you tell them what action you want them to take, having viewed your content.

- Be concise and make your call to action easy (no more than one sentence).
- If you want engagement, ask them to comment. If you want them to contact you, ask them to, and be specific about how they should (message, email, phone call, etc.).

> **Example Content**
>
> **Attention**
> Can I get a mortgage with one year's accounts?
>
> **Interest**
> If you are someone that has recently gone self-employed, it could be possible, depending on your individual circumstances. Getting a mortgage is like piecing together a puzzle. Everyone's puzzle is completely different, and there are a few things you need to know:
>
> - You need to have been trading for at least 12 months
> - Ideally, you want to make sure you've had experience in the trade beforehand.
> - You will need to either have accounts or tax computations and tax year overviews.
>
> **Desire**
> In terms of piecing this puzzle together, the best time you can start is now. You need to make sure that you start to get organised with this so you can buy your dream home as soon as possible.
>
> **Action**
> If you want help with this, make sure you comment below.

As you can see, the content doesn't need to be long. Break it into short sentences and paragraphs. Bullet points help massively.

NOW, CREATE YOUR CONTENT. MAKE IT EASY FOR YOUR CUSTOMER TO WATCH OR READ.

Attention	
Interest	
Desire	
Action	

> **NOTE**
> Before creating your content, close your eyes and picture your ideal client as a real person.
> Visualise their face, their dress sense, their mannerisms.
> Then imagine you are having a chat with them. Create your content in the same way you would speak to a friend about your chosen topic.

This works no matter the platform your content is on. It can be an email, a social post, a Facebook ad, even a written letter.

Building credibility

Do you believe you need more qualifications to attract more leads? That your leads are going to love your certificates and letters after your name? The people that will are in the minority.

If you love qualifications, learning, and doing exams then crack on – keep doing it. If it gives you more confidence and it's high on your values, keep doing it for yourself. I love learning and improving my skills, sharpening my sword, but no one has ever asked to see my qualifications in mortgage brokering, marketing, or coaching.

So, if knowledge isn't power and doesn't give you credibility, then what does?

Being the most known.

When people know who you are, they are more inclined

to buy from you and invest in your product or service. So, when building credibility, your focus is becoming the most known.

Joe Wicks (The Body Coach) isn't the best chef. He's actually not even a chef and yet he has some of the bestselling cookbooks of all time. Is he the best personal trainer? Probably not. But he is extremely likeable, lets people in to know who he is and he is the most known and, as a result, he has the largest fitness following online; he speaks, sells books, programs – he released "Wean in 15" for kids and it sold out. He built such a well-known brand by consistently creating content for his ideal client.

Your job is to become the most known in your niche, industry, town, county, postcode, country, even the world in what you do, sell, or offer. Sometimes it happens by accident and in the blink of an eye – it could take just one thing to make you go viral (I am yet to go viral, and I not bothered if I don't ever). More often, it takes years of consistently building your brand, improving your craft, and making marginal gains in your marketing skills to become an 'overnight success'.

Let's me stress, you do not need a huge social media following to generate leads. My social media following isn't massive, and yet what I do have is an engaged, loyal audience that knows, likes, and trusts me to buy my product and services.

This book is not about building a huge social media following, it's about building relationships and generating conversations with people that want to buy from you. The principles in this book and my small social media following have made my businesses over £5m in almost seven years with virtually zero spend on marketing tactics.

The best business owners are the best content marketers

Being a business owner has evolved dramatically. When I started my business in 2006, it was blood, sweat, and tears. When I started again in 2016, I put the same back into it and the hard work paid off.

But with the way of the world now, if you want a business to last—a profitable and fun lifestyle business, that is—then you need to understand digital marketing. The more you resist, the more certain you are to fail.

Technology has and is changing everything, including the way we all do business. We want speed, efficiency, and time saving. Look at Amazon revolutionising buying online with "one-click purchases" and man, do I spend a lot on Amazon; it's just the convenience of it.

Of course, your clients are all different, and one marketing message will not work on everyone. That is why it is vitally important to understand yourself and your audience when it comes to marketing because some like to watch, others read, while some will want to listen.

Your clients want to visualise the problem and possible solution (your offer), and the detail behind it. Understanding this makes it much easy to attract leads. We don't want all clients; we only want the ones who are perfect for our services or products.

If your clients can't find you, your product, or your services online while they are conducting research, they will find your competitor.

Consistent content marketing
Have a plan that you can stick to seven days a week. Having a content plan means you can focus every day and potentially prepare in advance to consistently market your business. Here's an example:

MONDAY	• Motivation • Mindset	Notes
TUESDAY	• Tips • Testimonials	Notes
WEDNESDAY	• Wisdom • Wins	Notes
THURSDAY	• Thoughts • Thankful	Notes
FRIDAY	• Fun Fact	Notes
SATURDAY	• Social • Selfie	Notes
SUNDAY	• Support • Solution	Notes

Whichever method you want to follow—whether it be watch, read, or listen—you can break down each day into what you love to produce. When you follow a winning recipe to bake a cake, you are guaranteed to end up with a beautiful dessert at the end of it. This is the exact same principle when you have a content marketing plan to follow.

A gift to help you be consistent

When you have a plan, it's easier to take action and remain consistent, which is the only thing that works. Knowing how hard this can be for so many business owners and advisers, I created **How To Generate Leads For Less**. It gives you 30 inspirational content ideas for the next 30 days to get more results. Make sure you download your free copy to help you get started:

https://30tips.theleadgenerationguide.co.uk

Repurposing content

One of the best methods for creating content is to turn one piece of long-form content into multiple pieces that you share throughout the week. As mentioned previously, your job is to create the content ideas and the original piece of content, thereafter you should not have any involvement, but you should be seen on social media every day.

Here's how this works for me:

1. Create 1-2 videos in 5 to 20 minutes per week, which will be edited and added to YouTube.
2. The audio will be stripped and uploaded to the podcast tool which puts it on every single channel.

3. The team will then take relevant comments, questions, statements, etc., and use these for TikTok/Reel/short-form video content.
4. Written content is created and shared on all social media channels, in Facebook groups, and email campaigns to promote the YouTube channel and Podcast.
5. Images are made to create thumbnails and for stories to drive people to watch, listen, or read all of the above.

I am a hugely process-driven person. Once you have a process in place that works, it can be systemised and leveraged to others who can take care of the '£10 tasks' – repurposing. This gives the impression that you are everywhere when, in fact, you are nowhere. Although, I still enjoy answering all the comments, messages, and DMs myself.

I realised the importance of repurposing back in 2016. With only six months of knowledge of social media and content marketing, I recruited an apprentice with one core skill: video editing. This one decision forced me to move from written posts and poor selfie images to creating consistent video to make sure the apprentice had some work to do. Over the years, we turned this process into a 7-figure business and income lead generator.

For you to begin repurposing, you must first decide what you will use to create your original piece of content: video, podcast, or blog.

The reason why I create video is because we can easily repurpose it into the other two. If you choose blog because you are an amazing writer, then it's near impossible to create the other two without extra work.

Remember, consistency is key, so make sure to begin with the one you can do consistently. If you enjoy the process, your content will get better, and once you are in a rhythm, it's much easier to begin repurposing your original content.

The process we have developed in my businesses is one that has been refined over the years and taught to many a business owner. It's also a service we have started to do for others in my agency and we get significant results.

Step 2 Actions

1. Create content using AIDA.
2. Create a content marketing plan.
3. Pick your main style of content – video, audio, or audio?
4. Create one piece of long-form content and repurpose it.

Notes

STEP 3
Social Media

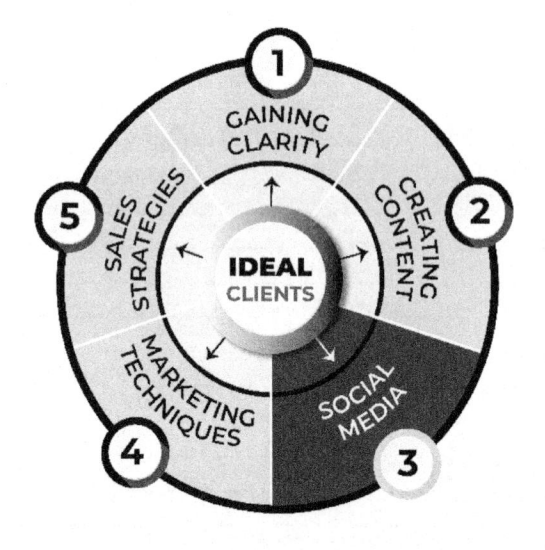

Back in 2015, I hated social media, so when I spotted a huge opportunity to utilise social media to generate clients within the mortgage industry, it's fair to say there was a lot of resistance.

- I didn't want people I know to know my business.
- I was worried that people would judge me.

- I didn't want to publish videos and I thought my content would be rubbish.

I'm sure these are things that have gone through your mind, too. It's natural. I'm not going to tell you to take a leap of faith because even though you will come to learn that those fears are irrational, they still create a mental block that may prevent you from ever taking that leap in the first place. Instead, I want to make three practical points that will help you overcome that fear.

Point #1: Social media isn't the only way to generate clients.

If you really don't want to do social media or you don't like a particular social platform, no problem.

Point #2: Create 'business-only' profiles for yourself.

I think the biggest fear people have is judgment from their social circle (friends, family, and acquaintances). The simple way around that is to create social media profiles where you're not connected to any of these people. Just your ideal client.

Point #3: Content comes in many forms.

There's a perception that I *make* my students publish videos, but that isn't the case. It is, however, the fastest way to get traction online and seems to keep growing.

I do video because it's what I'm best at. But for you, it might be that you're better at writing or that you are a good speaker and podcasts are your thing. The key is to find something that works for you to get you started because once you start, you'll wonder what the worry was all about. In fact, you'll probably kick yourself for not starting sooner because the opportunity is enormous.

In 2016, I thought social media was full of woe-is-me stories and cats on skateboards. But then I noticed how fitness influencers were using it to generate leads for free. That was a real lightbulb moment because nobody in financial services was doing it.

But spotting the opportunity was only one-tenth of the battle. The real challenge was actually getting started. And to tell you the truth, I was nervous about putting myself out there. The thought of posting something and sharing my expertise felt like a vulnerable position to be in.

- Would people judge me?
- Would I get trolled?
- Or will I just get ignored?

I know full well that this is something that's holding you back, too. But learning how to connect with clients online is vital for your brand because your clients are on their mobiles and social media channels every day. Physical events are still important, but so are online events such as webinars.

Making sure that you hit the watch, read, and listen with videos, blogs, and a podcast is going to give your clients more chance of choosing your brand over others. Having a website is simply not enough anymore and if you want to compete in your local area or nationally, you need social media channels to market your brand and use them to your advantage.

Using social media to help build your brand has countless advantages:

- Show off your brand
- Build deeper relationships
- Get more people to know, like, and trust you
- Increase your leads and sales
- Get client feedback
- Improve your Google results
- Reduce your marketing spend

Social media is free to use, and there are so many organic methods you can use to generate leads and traction for your business. Not to mention the number of social media users is continuing to grow year-on-year. Being on social media can:

- Increase your email open rates
- Boost traffic to your website
- Improve your word of mouth
- Increase event attendance

We can go a layer deeper with each of the above to improve your marketing efforts:

- The "call to action" text in your email will have a bigger impact on conversions.
- The "call to action" you use on social media will drive more traffic.
- The language you use will make more clients want to refer you.

Occasionally on social media (often if you are polarising), you may receive negative feedback. If this happens, there are a variety of ways to manage it and how to manage it will depend on the post. Was it business or personal? Is it a customer or just someone being negative? Just remember the term "keyboard warrior" – people can be a lot braver when they are protected by a screen. Do not let this small potential fear stop you from taking control of your lead generation.

It's time to embrace social media, but it takes much more than creating a profile, page, or group to successfully grow your brand. You need a strategy to use it effectively, efficiently, and most importantly, to monetise it. You need to learn the strategies to build your brand and separate yourself from everyone else in your industry so it's you potential clients want to buy from.

This is not an easy task; it took me years and plenty of investment in courses and mentors to learn and invent the process I share in this book. Without goals and a proper plan, you will get mediocre results, you will continue to waste time, and have a leaky bucket in your marketing.

But growing your brand on social media isn't just about finding new clients, it's also about retaining previous ones. Using groups to build communities of like-minded people is a powerful strategy that we'll dive into later.

Being a business owner has changed and it is going to continue to change. The one constant is that social media and digital marketing are always evolving and if you adapt to the new trends as they come, you will thrive and have a competitive advantage over faceless national brands.

You do not need to be an expert at coding a website, you can hire someone to do that. But you do need to become an expert at all the free "organic" methods of growing your brand and generating leads, clients, and sales online.

Size doesn't matter

Your social media results have absolutely nothing to do with the size of your audience because 90% of people will never engage (like, comment or share) with you anyway. But your ideal client is always watching.

It's much better to have a small and engaged audience than hundreds of 1000s of followers for vanity metrics. I see it all the time on Instagram; an influencer will have 150k followers and a post with five likes and ten views.

One of the big realisations I've had in building my social media audience since March of 2019 is that advisers aren't going to generally like, comment, or share my posts. The reason being is this will result in them sharing it with their competition. By keeping it to themselves they (and maybe you) believe they have the upper hand and an advantage by holding onto the knowledge I am sharing about generating leads, increasing sales, and maximising profit.

At this time, my social media following (rounded) is:

- 6.8K Facebook profile
- 10K Facebook
- 1.9K Instagram
- 13.5K LinkedIn
- 3.6K subscribers on YouTube
- 5K PRO Podcast downloads per month
- 6K email database
- 3.8K across two Facebook groups
- **TOTAL 50.6K**

For example purposes, if 10% agree to purchase something

I offer at £1,000, then that's £5.06m turnover and as the audience grows that amount will increase. I only emphasise that to you because no matter how big your following right now, if you can convert just 10%, you have a business and you can begin to work out how much every fan, follower or subscriber could be worth to you.

If you choose to focus on a specific niche, whatever it may be—mortgages, property investment, potato recipes, life hacks—then your following has a higher chance of expanding.

In summary, size doesn't matter; it's about niche, connection, relationships, and providing value to your audience consistently. Most business owners give up too early and forget that's it showing up *consistently* that works. The compound effect of small daily actions over time will generate more leads for your business, providing you are leveraging all the elements in this book.

Which channel is best?

One question that always gets asked is what social media platform should I be on? Simple answer – all of them. Even as new platforms open, register to secure your username to stay consistent in your personal and business brands across all channels.

I hope by now you understand the power of social media and the need to be famous to a few. We aren't talking millions and millions of clients (unless that is your goal), but 1000 loyal fans spending £1,000 gives you a solid business for the future.

Social media isn't going anywhere for a long time, so

you need to start taking it seriously and using it as part of your marketing strategy. I have spoken about why you should be on it, now I want to give you some strategies for each channel you need to be on.

One of the key considerations when choosing a primary channel is who your client is because your ideal client may not be on your favourite channel, which would just mean wasting most of your efforts.

There are entire books written on each of the social media channels I am about to mention, so I'm not going to give you War and Peace on each. I am going to share with you the ones I spend time on, how I have used them, and give you ideas about what you can use them for, too.

Social media made easy

How many times have you logged into social media with the intention of being productive and, all of a sudden, you are watching TikTok dances? An hour has gone by, and you've been consuming instead of creating.

Don't worry, we've all done it. TikTok is one that I can lose some serious time on, it's a nightmare. But that's a big element of social media – escapism. Many of your clients turn to social media to escape the day-to-day. They are there as a lurker, consuming instead of creating, and this is why social platforms are so powerful and so effective as a tool to generate leads.

There are four main ways to gain attention with your content:

1. Educate
2. Entertain

3. Inspire
4. Evoke emotion

If you can do all four with your content, then you have the golden goose. For me, it was difficult to entertain clients when talking about mortgages, which is why personal branding was so important. TikTok has now changed that and brought about "edutainment" (educational, entertaining content).

An important element of content marketing and social media is making your audience feel something. Playing on your audience's emotion grabs attention and gains engagement. Many do this via polarisation, sharing an opinion that may be controversial or different from the norm. When your posts get people talking in the comments, good or bad, it builds traction.

The most important thing is to be the real you when producing content; your mannerisms, how animated you are, the language you use, and the passion you put into your content come across, no matter the industry you're in.

Remember, your emphasis should be on having fun with it. It may be a chore or challenge when you first start out, and you'll no doubt have thoughts like:

- Will people criticise me?
- Does my hair look good?
- I have a huge spot on my cheek right now.
- I'm rubbish at writing, my English is bad, my grammar is poor, I always forget 'your' and 'you're'.
- I just don't have anything to say.

All these statements will ring through your head when you start, but just *start*. Most of the world and your clients are too concerned with their own life to notice your fears and anxieties.

There are some questions to ask yourself when embarking on your social media journey, even if you are already using it and getting little traction…

How do you stay productive on social media?

Productivity is imperative, so how do you make sure you get results? Do you measure leads, engagement, "reach", comments, followers? Start with your intention and then you can be aware of your behaviours to ensure success.

You must switch your mind from consumption to creation. Remember, everything you do, see, hear, and feel could technically become content.

The easiest method I have for staying productive is creating a consistent routine for posting in the morning and a separate time for engaging (usually lunch time and in the afternoon). This means when I log into a social media channel, it's with an intention and not just for consumption. If I am researching ideas, it's because I have added that time to my diary to complete that task.

How do you maximise the time you spend on social media?

As you begin to be productive on social media and start to see results, you move from creating to documenting. This is a method spoken about by Gary Vaynerchuk and it links into the above question.

> **Gary Vaynerchuk (Gary Vee)**
> I call him the Godfather of social media and personal brand. First known as a wine critic who expanded his family's wine business, Vaynerchuk is now more known for his work in digital marketing and social media as the chairman of New York-based communications company VaynerX, and as CEO of VaynerX subsidiary VaynerMedia.

You'll start with creating specific content for your client. It will be structured, maybe scripted, and usually planned. But as your confidence grows, you will become freer with it, and it will become easier; you'll think less about what to create and begin to see content everywhere.

Documenting your "daily life" is about sharing stories, updates, and value as it happens. Through your day, there are lessons, education, entertainment, and emotional triggers that people will be able to relate to. If ever you think you don't have anything to post, think about what you are doing right now.

For example, take a picture of you holding this book and share it on your social media with the caption: *"I'm improving my lead generation knowledge to attract better quality clients; my biggest take away from the book so far is xyz – what was the last book you read?"*

Everyone loves to comment and share their favourite books, and I have no doubt this type of post will do well because others can relate and engage, plus you gain new ideas for books to read.

How to automate your social media
There are two options for posting on social media:

1. You/your team physically post on the channel via phone, tablet or computer (typing the post, uploading your video, etc.).
2. Using a scheduling software like Hootsuite, Buffer or Creator Studio, which is the Facebook and Instagram scheduling tool.

My team and I tend not to use any automation tools when sharing. For the minimal time it takes to post, we find that our reach (total number of people who see the post) is generally higher with more engagement when doing it ourselves. If you struggle with being consistent or want to post at a time of day that is convenient for you, starting with a scheduling tool could help. As with most things in marketing, it should involve testing and measuring for you and your audience.

How do you repurpose to be everywhere?
As one person, you can only do so much. To reach more clients and get more leads, you need to let go to grow. Your goal is not to give up doing the content (as I have said before), instead, your job is to get better at the content and then hire someone on your team or get a VA who can take that one piece of content and share it far and wide.

When you do start hiring, your second or third team member should be a social media manager, marketing apprentice, or VA. In 2016 after only 6 months of using social for lead generation I employed my first apprentice to help with sharing that content far and wide, this decision increase the ideal clients and increased my sales.

How do you grow your platforms?

As your content moves from one channel to multiple, your content will no doubt improve. Your next goal is to look at the analytics and insights to track what is and isn't working. It's about putting a little more effort into the assessment to increase your results.

80% of your results come from 20% of your effort, so you need to find that sweet spot by testing new channels and styles. Doing the same thing for too long can be good for consistency but it can also be a hindrance.

Each social media channel also has trends (a sound on TikTok, an image style on Instagram, etc.). Stay on top of the latest trends to ride the wave that could grow your audience.

A great website to stay on top of the latest trends is https://www.socialmediatoday.com/

Your social media landing page

Don't underestimate the power of your social media profiles. Your potential clients Google you because they want to know who you are; they are lurking and observing to see if you are consistent and showing up or if you are giving up at the first hurdle.

One of the most powerful methods of getting leads is thinking of your profile or page as a website. When someone searches you or goes to find out more, what do they see?

- In the first few posts, are they seeing content that is relevant to them or are they seeing you drunk in a nightclub? (Unless you're a club promoter, then this may be what you want them to see).
- When they look at your images (yes, a lot of clients will do that), what are they seeing?
- When they see your profile image, is it you or an irrelevant picture of your kids, the dog, or worse, just a random image?
- Are your website and links to relevant pages of authority up to date?
- Is your bio on point so it attracts interest?

Think like a client and these minor tweaks can see huge improvements in the results you get.

One question that always comes up when I am teaching social media is, *what do I do about my friends and family? They don't want to see my business stuff.* There is an element of fear behind what they might say. Another common question is, *I have old uni pictures, should I start a new profile?*

I can tell you this now: your friends and family will be the last ones to like, comment, and share. But they will be the first to call you out, criticise, and ask what you are doing. Who cares? They aren't your client anyway.

One of my team recently did her first video and it was good. I showed my wife and she said, "it's really good, better than your first one." Cheers. Ayesha (my wife) couldn't watch any of my first ones without cringing.

Your partner will be almost as big a critic as you just because they know you better than anyone else and, to be honest, because they aren't the ones doing it. Maybe they don't even get why you're doing it. In reality, Ayesha is my best friend, incredibly supportive, and she is critical because she loves me and wants to help me improve. Her initial thoughts motivated me even more to get better.

I believe the decision you first need to make is, if you want to use social media for lead generation? Or do you want to use it to stay connected to your friends? I made the decision that my friends are in my WhatsApp and went with lead generation.

Video: Live or prerecord?
When I started using social media in 2016, all I did was post once per day. Then I joined a group for £97 a month because they had a big focus on teaching social media over three months. It was my first investment in online courses, training, and even a mentor.

Within three months, I was posting pictures, writing better content, getting more engagement, and by June, I had done my first video. Back then, there were virtually no advisers using content marketing, especially video. I started to share one pre-recorded video per week about a specific mortgage topic and I couldn't watch any of my early ones out of fear. But it made no difference, and it actually started to generate leads.

It doesn't matter what you choose to do, the main thing is just doing it. If you aren't confident going live, then do pre-recorded content first. I like to mix it up based on the purpose of the video and the result I want to get from it.

You also don't have to do video at all – plenty of clients like to listen and read. But if you want to leverage your time and repurpose the most content, video will eventually become a must.

What are #tags?
#justsaying #winning #getshitdone #garydas #entrepreneur #author #photooftheday #essex #mortgagebroker #businesscoach #socialmedia #prosocialmedia #leadgenerationguide

These are just a few examples of #tags and their purpose is to put your posts, pictures, videos, or images into categories. On some social media channels, these are a must for growth and increased following. Some of your clients will use these to search for similar posts, so when you use a #tag and someone searches that #tag, your post has a chance of showing up to them, which could mean more reach, engagement, and results.

It's like going to Google images and searching "entrepreneur"; what Google shows you is based on that "keyword", and a #tag is just a keyword.

With the algorithm constantly changing, you need to surround yourself with social media experts who know what changes are happening so you can adjust your strategy and your actions accordingly.

There is plenty of information available online to keep yourself up to speed on one social media channel. You can be self-taught, just remember that learning through trial and error can be more time consuming and, therefore, more costly.

The algorithm
Every social media channel has an algorithm. It's like the

matrix; it controls what you see, which of your friends see your posts, and it means that you only have a percentage of control over what is in your feed.

The problem is that every channel is constantly changing its algorithm, so what works one day may not work the next. There are ways in which you can game the algorithm and use it to your advantage but in most cases, the only way to know is to test.

Everything about social media is a test because of this. The social media channels have their own goals and agenda for how they want you to behave and act. They have control over what should and shouldn't do well based on their goals, which can add a little frustration to the results you can get, but it's also part of the fun.

Remember, when using social media for business to build know, like, and trust to generate leads, clients, and sales, you are not making content for yourself, you are making it for your audience. The algorithm (depending on the channel) has so much data on every single person; it knows what people want to see, or at least it thinks it does.

Social Media Tip

If you like something, the algorithm will show you more of that stuff. If you don't engage, like, comment, or interact with something or someone, it won't show you them anymore. So, if you see stuff on a daily basis that you don't like – unfollow, unfriend and engage with more of what you want to see.

Are you a lurker?

At some stage you have been, without a shadow of a doubt, we all have. There have been times when you've seen a post you liked, you may have even read the comments, but you didn't like, comment, or share the post yourself.

Everyone has done it, and the scary thing is, the majority of clients do the same. It's been banded around that as much as 90% of clients will never do any of those three and just lurk in the shadows, watching you and observing, building this value pot of know, like, and trust.

Some people don't like leaving comments because they don't want to be judged or they don't want to be wrong. Then, one day, you get this magical message in your DMs... *"I've been watching you."*

Yes, they literally say that and yes, it is a little bit weird. But then they follow up with:

- I love your content...
- I've seen your journey...
- Thank you for...

Any number of niceties followed by *"I want to buy your product/service."*

You have never seen them before, you have never had any interaction, and yet they have this complete faith in you to solve their problem. You have taken them from attention to interest to desire and now to action. And you didn't even know it was happening.

Unbeknown to you, you have been filling up their value pot slowly over time with your content, consistency, and personality, helping you stand out to them and making you their logical choice.

Your blind faith in posting on social media suddenly pays off big time because when that happens, they will literally pay whatever you want to charge. That client is your biggest fan, they have been on a journey with you, and they want to, no, they *must* use your services. Now your efforts are being rewarded and your opportunity has just doubled.

That is the power of blind faith and playing the long game in what I am teaching you here. Your mission is to create that again and again and it always comes right back to asking yourself, who is your ideal client you want to work with five days per week and 52 weeks of the year?

Social media is about connection, networking, and building your audience, so that you earn the right to be able to sell your products and services. I have shared some key insights into the channels I use and find to be most effective, but there are many other channels you can use, and you should investigate if they suit your style.

The size of your following does not matter and will grow organically over time. When I started out in 2016, I had zero social media presence or following. I also only focused on one social media channel to generate leads. As I increased my sales and made more profit, I reinvested into my marketing so that I could repurpose my content across other channels and be more omnipresent at any point in time. I also started introducing my podcast in 2019 and putting more energy and effort into YouTube.

Everything that we have discussed so far is about the fundamental building blocks. It's about working out one method that you can be consistent with, mastering that one method, making money from that one method, and then beginning to grow.

You are at the base of a mountain and each time you step up to a new level, you're going to add something new. The compound effect of generating leads, increasing sales, and maximising profit will lead to a more successful business, giving you more time to do what you love with who you love.

Social proof

There is one type of content that generally gets better results on social media than any other and that is social proof. Here's how social proof is described on Wikipedia:

> *"Social proof is a psychological phenomenon where people assume the actions of others in an attempt to reflect correct behaviour for a given situation."*

Robert Cialdini, who talks about the principle of social proof in-depth in his book, *Influence: The Psychology of Persuasion*, says, "We view a behaviour as more correct in a given situation to the degree that we see others performing it."

In short, share:

1. Case studies
2. Testimonials and reviews
3. Existing customers and clients
4. Awards and accolades

5. User-generated content (and get your clients to share yours on their channels)

In marketing, when people shop, they look for reviews, recommendations, and ways that others have used a product or service before making their decision, so make sure you are including it in your content strategy.

Step 3 Actions

1. Choose one social media channel and post consistently, preferably daily.
2. Assess the analytics and produce better content based on engagement.
3. Set up your social media landing pages with relevant links, images, and social proof.
4. Find #tags related to your niche.

Notes

STEP 4
Marketing Techniques

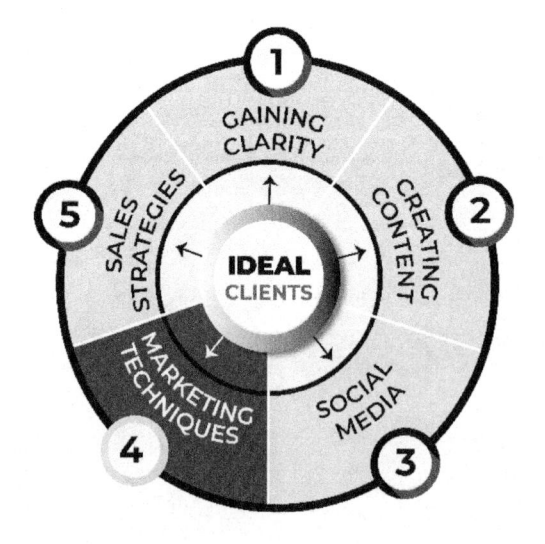

Taking clients away from social media

Dani is a photographer who spent five years building his Instagram account to promote his business. During those five years of hard work and dedication to the platform, he amassed 135,000 followers. But one day, he went to log into his account and saw nine words that made his heart sink:

> *"Your account has been disabled for violating our terms."*

He combed through the terms of service word-by-word but couldn't find a single rule that he was in violation of. When he reached out to Instagram, his appeals fell on deaf ears. People in his community suggested that he had fallen foul to rival businesses reporting his page for no reason other than to remove him as competition.

Imagine that. You pour your blood, sweat, and tears into building an audience on a platform, only for it to go up in smoke overnight. And that's not the only danger, either. Since 2016, I've built a decent-sized engaged following on Facebook. My posts used to get a huge number of views and lots of interaction. Over time, we've increased the production value of the content and its quality. So, our views should be increasing, right? Not the case.

I've watched my reach decline over time. Facebook sought to drive bigger profits by adjusting the algorithm. There's no such thing as a free lunch, and Facebook wanted to encourage businesses to spend money on ads. I've seen similar changes occur on LinkedIn and Instagram, too, and I've no doubt that one day, it'll be much harder going.

There will always be a way you can use these platforms to grab attention. But those methods can change with the wind, and you have to stay alert. This is a very important lesson for anyone who uses social media to market their business.

Don't get me wrong, I remain a huge advocate of using social media. It's my thing, and I owe a lot to it. But you must view each of these platforms as a tool to use as part of your wider marketing strategy. Devise ways to move your audience from the platforms to assets you own, such as an email list.

If you rely on one platform, you're an algorithm change or an account suspension away from disaster. That's why social media forms one component of my effective marketing strategy, which I'm in full control of.

Direct response vs. brand marketing

Direct response marketing aims to close a sale right then and there. Brand marketing, on the other hand, is a longer play. It is everything we have been discussing in this book so far. You are building brand equity which is building value in the minds of your ideal clients.

I am a huge fan of doing both. Brand marketing will attract deeper-spending clients, but they take longer to convert into sales. Direct response marketing, such as an ad on Google or Facebook, gives you the chance to make sales quicker, but you have to know your numbers, the terminology, and how to effectively run ads to get clear results. We will cover this in this section.

A lead is not a lead

When I started my business back in 2006—and up until 2015—I bought 1000s of leads a year. At my peak with a team of 13, I was spending £250,000 on poor quality leads that got worse over time to support my business. It was a vicious cycle and a trap I couldn't get out of.

As the mortgage and insurance industry began to change, the cost-per-lead remained the same, but the conversion percentage began to reduce. It then became highly unpredictable – one month could mean 30% conversion, the next it could be 10%. It was taking more time to manage the sales team (insurance advisers) and more time to assess each lead, and I am very confident it was because:

1. The lead providers were multi-selling the leads to double their income, which created more competition.
2. Due to more competition, my competitor was sacrificing commission to be more competitively priced to win the deal.

I began to hate my business, I felt huge anxiety and stress every day, but I didn't know any other way out of the trap I had created for myself.

Buy leads, make sales, and repeat.

For every lead that came in, our goal was to speak to someone, but we probably ended up speaking to 50% because of the poor quality. If you're buying leads, you're probably experiencing that as well; you just get ghosted – money and time wasted trying to make contact.

Today, I would not call this a lead. The part involving a conversation I call a strategy call or discovery call. You might pay £50 or £60, and you may speak to one in every two, depending on the source. But these clients are in the action phase which, remember from earlier, is the smallest part of the sales funnel.

Today, a *lead* is getting a client into your database (i.e., onto your email list where you now own their information). This gives you the ability to build a better relationship with them and find out what they are truly interested in. Email marketing tools can tell you what they open, click on, and even gives your leads a score.

This type of lead can cost you £2.00 to £15.00, depending on the strategy you use to convert clients from social media or paid ads. Not every single one will want to speak to you now, and the likelihood is the majority are in the attention, interest, or desire phase. But you'll have at least 10x the opportunity to make a conversion, and with 10x the opportunity, you only need 10% to actually convert to paying clients. You'll also have 10x the opportunity for referrals and recommendations.

How many times have you had a referral or recommendation from someone you have never directly done business with before? Once someone becomes a lead, you are now more connected, you are delivering valuable information through your email marketing database, your emails could even be being forwarded without your knowledge (which is more valuable than a social media share).

Some say email is dead, I completely disagree:

- For my mortgage business, our recent research showed a conversion rate of 17.6% from clients who had downloaded our eBook.
- From a £1,543 spend on Facebook ads and 1,143 leads on our database, we generated 30 sales valued at £37,835.76.
- In my training business, even with scheduled posts in Facebook groups and on my social media channels, 48 of 53 sign-ups were through email.

- Email is a deeper connection with your client. Generally, they don't miss an email, whereas your client may only see 50% of your social media posts due to the algorithm, the time of day you post, when they are online, etc.

Google My Business (GMB)

GMB is a form of brand marketing. When someone sees you or your business on social media, there is a good chance they will go to Google (or YouTube) and search for you. GMB is free to use and helps local businesses get higher visibility in Google searches. It's a great way to build up a local presence for *free*.

When you optimise your GMB listing, your page can help your business stand out against your competitors in your local area. It also gives you the chance to start collecting Google reviews. And the more space you occupy on the web, especially on Google Search, the more chances of your prospective clients buying from you.

Including GMB in your marketing strategy is essential for a number of reasons:

- Local SEO
- Collecting reviews
- Business information gathered directly from the search engine
- Marketing and communication
- Google My Business Insights and its benefits for analytics
- Free of cost
- Ease of use

You can get higher up the ranking in your business's

local area by optimising your local SEO, so make sure you get your GMB set up ASAP.

Building your email list
This is where you really make sales in your business, and I'm not talking about the physical conversation of "buy my stuff" or money exchanging hands – that's not the world we live in anymore thanks to social media and buying choices, as I explained earlier.

The sales I am talking about in this section involve moving potential clients from social media into your world so you can build a closer and more connected relationship with them (i.e., generating a lead) – this is step one of your sales process.

Step two of your sales process is getting them to book a call with you or one of your sales team.

Step three would be making the physical sale and the exchange of money.

There are sub-steps between the above; in the mortgage world, for example, between two and three there is awaiting documents, a fact-finding call, assessment, sending illustrations, agreement in principles, and possibly more depending on your business model.

If you are in a product-based business, then you will get clients who impulse buy or don't need to take the extra step (online sales is slightly different). But if you are selling a £2,000 product, that is completely different from selling a £50 impulse product, so adding this chapter into your sales process is vital.

If you do step one correctly, steps two and three are

simple. You are no longer selling because your clients come to you pre-sold. So, think about how you can pre-sell your clients when creating your customer journey.

Landing pages

Your website is about brand awareness, and in an ideal world, your website will take your lead on a journey to learn more about your business and the services you provide. At the top of your website, you have 'options' – home, about, services, testimonials, contact – for leads to find out more.

Too many options can lead to inaction, whereas a landing page removes the options. It has one single focus – to click a button to submit their details. In my businesses, we use landing pages for eBooks, events, and, most certainly, for ads.

A single focus means more results, i.e., leads.

Thank you pages

"Thank you" pages are the perfect opportunity to invite your lead to take next steps with you. 100% of the people who have given you their contact details are going to land on the thank you page hoping to see what has been promised. If your niche is clear and your messaging strong, then every visitor sent to the thank you page should be your ideal client.

This means you can offer them something on the thank you page. For example, book a call with you, an invite to a webinar, or free training. Maximise the offer here to give you the highest chance of conversion to sale.

Lead capture

Bribery – *I'll give you this if you give me that*. Here is something of value for you in exchange for your email address and phone number and the ability to keep emailing you every week with value, information, and occasional offers.

Remember, watch, read, and listen are the three ways your clients like to take in content. In this sales method, we can also add "Do" to the list. Clients like to do some work; complete a workbook, answer a quiz, take a challenge – these are methods that build a better connection.

eBook

An eBook is a bribery tool, they come in all shapes and sizes, from a one-page PDF to a 15,000-word book. The most important thing about using an eBook to capture your client's email and phone number is giving them something of value, something to solve a pain, educate them, and build your credibility.

I absolutely love eBook marketing. You can use Facebook ads to target an audience and get downloads from £1.50 to £15.00, depending on your product or service. When you provide something of low cost and high value, your client will be blown away. Solve a problem and give them some action steps to complete but also educate them on how you want them to behave or act, so your client comes to you ready to do business.

Once your client has downloaded your eBook from your website or third-party landing page, you'll need a sequence of emails to give them even more value; a video link on

YouTube, a podcast episode, a Facebook group, even a small offer for something low-cost to remove the friction of purchasing your main product.

I want to bring you back to the value pot your client is building in their mind through the journey they have been on with you:

- Free content on social media
- Consistently adding free value
- Occasionally pitching and making offers
- Giving them an eBook *technically* for free but in exchange for an email and/or phone number

They now have a lot of know, like, and trust for you, your brand, your product, or service. So, nudging them along to the buying conversation when you make them an offer is so much easier.

Webinars

A webinar is an online presentation where you can have real-time conversations with 100s or 1000s of people, depending on the platform. The ability to speak one-to-many is so powerful for your product or service and your closing call-to-action should be to take the next logical step (book a strategy or discover call or even buy your product or service).

You can use your webinar to attract new clients, remarket to eBook downloads, even sell to existing clients. Your webinar can be a couple of hours long or even an entire day. At the beginning of Covid-19, I held a two-hour Survive and Thrive webinar for advisers to help them plan for the new world. In May of 2020, I held the first

"Financial PRO Online Summit" which was a free event delivered inside one of my *PRO Communities* on Facebook. I had six of the best speakers covering every aspect of building your financial services business. We had approximately 750 advisers join our database and more than 350 online all day from 10 am to 6 pm.

A compelling webinar needs to have a clear objective, goal, or outcome, even a problem it can solve for your attendee. This goes right back to your client and making sure you know your audience so the topics you choose to discuss resonate with them.

Once you have chosen your subject and date for your webinar, there are just five steps to make it happen:

1. **Promotion** – get attention for your webinar and clients registered.
2. **Design** – the number of slides is roughly 30-50% of the number of minutes you want to speak for (e.g., 60 minutes = 18 to 30 slides).
3. **Practice** – make sure you have a good flow and allow ten minutes at the end to pitch the next steps.
4. **Platform** – you can use specific webinar software like Goto Webinar, do a Facebook Live, or use a presentation tool like Zoom or Stream Yard to go live in multiple places.
5. **Email sequence** – set up one for three days before and one for three days after because you'll always have fewer attendees than registrants.

Conversion from your webinar to the next steps will depend on the product or service and offer, but the beauty is when clients register and don't attend, you can still build more rapport through your email marketing.

If you want to attend any of my free trainings to see them in action, make sure you follow me on social media @garydas, especially Instagram, as I'm always promoting them there.

Quiz or scorecard

A quiz is a great way to promote engagement with you, your brand, and business. Customers love a quiz if it can offer them a result. As humans, we naturally place everything into categories, so a quiz appeals to most.

There are different types of quizzes you can run; I'll share the three I find most useful:

- A score – we naturally want to self-evaluate and compare ourselves to others to understand our opinions and abilities in certain areas.
- A killer – focuses on the fear of loss because clients are more inclined to move away from pain than they are towards the promise of gain, success, or results.
- A general survey – gain some valuable insight into your clients and where they are now. This one doesn't give the client a result like the other two, but when positioned correctly, it can help you to work out what your clients need and want.

If you have seen *The Great Hack* on Netflix (if you haven't, go watch it), you will know the level of data Facebook holds on everyone who logs into the platform. It can tell almost everything about you, using the algorithm to show you what it thinks you want to see. With Facebook or YouTube ads, you can target the tiniest detail about your client with a message specific to them about your product or service.

Data on your clients and their habits is key in the attention phase, so building in methods of capturing their contact details is important. The three lead magnet ideas we've discussed here can be used together as part of an automated email sequence or independently marketed organically or with Facebook ads.

For example, you could have a lead magnet eBook that drives them to a quiz that takes them into one of two webinars, based on their results. This is how you build an automated lead generation machine business with clients who love the value you bring into their world.

Automated email marketing

As I mentioned earlier in the book, email is far from dead as a marketing technique. It enables you to have better interactions with your clients and give value to them directly. You can segment your data and know who has opened emails, clicked links, or watched a video, which is awesome for retargeting and giving specific messages to your clients based on their interests and wants.

The goal of automated emails is to drive people to act or take the next logical step that you want them to take. But just using the lead magnets above isn't enough – you need a pre-planned sequence of emails that pushes them to take the action you want.

When you add someone new to your email list from a capture form on your website, you need some kind of introduction sequence to welcome them, give them value, and make them want to stay (it also doesn't hurt to remind them to add you to the safe senders list, so you don't get lost in the spam folder).

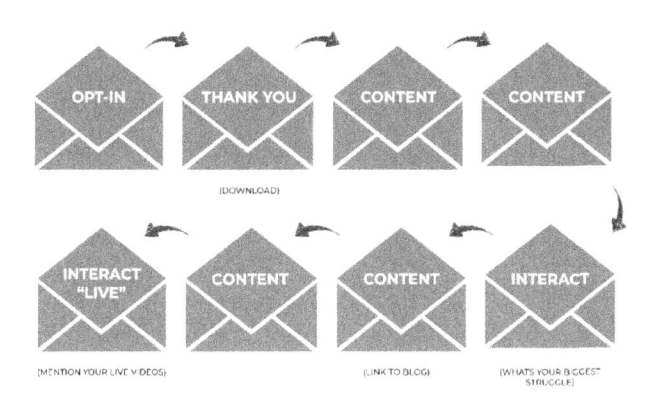

An automated sequence requires two-to-five emails that educate your lead on what they can expect by joining your newsletter.

Email 1
Deliver what you promised and tell your audience what they can expect from you. Share when you publish blog posts or podcasts and maybe even when you're doing a live video on social media. It should also detail what you plan on doing with your new subscriber's email address (i.e., set the expectation for what is to come).

Email 2
Tell them about your story and how you arrived where you're at.

Email 3
Tell them what you stand for and what you're against.

Emails 4-6
Share some of your best content that will resonate with them.

Email 7 - it's time for the offer
Address their pain points, talk about the benefits of your product, or whatever it is that you offer.

Your clients still use email every day. It may be secondary to their mobile phone, but much like the mobile phone, pretty much everyone has an email address. The problem for most business owners is they just don't know how to get email marketing right.

Clients get bombarded with emails all the time—spam, sales, and adverts—it's important to remember the "value first" method. The more value you provide to a client, the more you earn the right to pitch your product or service. If you're going to get in the habit of selling often, try to put yourself in your client's shoes – how much is too much? This will depend on the frequency of your emails. Try to send at least one a month, with one a week being your goal.

We find sending a mix of stories, case studies, value, and newsletter-style updates works really well. To maximise your opportunity with email, use an email marketing system to give you clear Key Performance Indicators (KPIs) and outcomes from your clients' email interactions. The advantage is the ability to use segmentation and access analytics to improve your messages and generate better results.

The three main metrics to track on your emails are:

- Open rate – how many clients have opened the email.
- Click-through rate – how many clients clicked on a link in the email.
- Unsubscribes – clearly, they have ditched you and you weren't adding value.

If you have a low click-through rate, it means your message was not good enough to hold your clients' attention and you need to improve your content.

Don't get hung up on the number of unsubscribes, providing they don't exceed your opt-in rate. You want more clients joining than leaving, so if the balance has swung the other way, then you have some serious work to do on adding value and writing good content.

When setting up an automated sequence after your lead magnet, assess where in the funnel leads are leaking out – where are your clients leaving your initial sequence? Knowing this gives you the ability to tweak (remember the marginal gains ethos).

Segmentation plays a huge part in your automated sequences because you can serve your audience with a clear message based on their interests or products they do not have. For example, knowing who doesn't have income protection and is self-employed is a great campaign we have running in my mortgage brokerage.

If you want to bring real value to your business, your email list is a great way to do it. You own the data and will be able to analyse stats for conversions from email marketing, cost per opt-in vs sales value, and lifetime client value.

This predictable income stream is a worthy investment for any adviser. How much is every subscriber worth to your business?

Running profitable ads
This is the last piece of the puzzle in the marketing step – maximising the effectiveness of your sales and giving you the opportunity to make it a predictable income stream. Everything we have spoken about until now costs you nothing other than your time or possibly the cost of a marketing consultant, apprentice, or social media manager. But the methods we have discussed have all been organic.

From 2016 until January 2020, I did not use Facebook ads other than a £2,500 test budget after investing in courses. I wanted to cement my education and, on reflection, I wish I had started sooner.

In this section, I cannot teach you how to run your ads, but I will give you my experience and how I use ads to drive more leads into my business in a consistent and low-cost way. I recommend learning how to do it before recruiting an ads manager or an agency to run your account for you. You cannot manage what you do not know how to measure. You must have a basic understanding of ads because a team will be spending your money to make it work.

If you choose to hire me and my team to run your ads, cool, it will be a pleasure.

I've spoken to many advisers, self-employed business owners, and even marketers who say Facebook ads don't work. When I investigate with some questions, it turns out they are running the wrong type of strategy for that platform.

You can run ads on Facebook, Instagram, Google, YouTube, LinkedIn, TikTok, the list goes on. You can get ultra-targeted on your niche and find ways to reach your clients by being clever with your keywords. But I'm going to share with you a simple strategy that you can use to drive more leads at a low cost, and for the purposes of this book, I am only going to reference Facebook, which includes Instagram since they run from the same ads manager platform.

Facebook ads are a powerful way to drive more traffic to your content and organic efforts. The great thing about Facebook is the level of data they hold about your lead. You can be so specific with who you want to target that you can drive your ideal client directly to your content and your eBook, quiz, or webinar.

What gets measured gets managed – your job is to understand enough to get results.

On Facebook: Do not press the Boost button

The big blue button that appears on your posts and the emails you receive from Facebook stating "this post is doing better than 80% of posts" is not the most efficient way to gain followers, fans, subscribers, and leads for your business.

The issue with this method is Facebook chooses the audience and the targeting, which means that your results will be less than ideal. The age demographic, for example, will be 18-65, which may not be your target market. By using Facebook ads and the business manager tool, you can be very specific with your ads to get maximum results.

So, let me share the must-know elements of Facebook ads with you.

Ads glossary

Here is a basic overview of some of the keywords. There is a lot of data available to you, and it's important to know what you are looking for and where it fits into the funnel.

- **Ad spend:** Amount you have spent on the ad
- **Impressions:** number of times your ad has been seen
- **Reach:** number of people who have seen your ad
- **Relevance:** a quality score based on the engagement that your ad receives
- **CPM (cost per mille):** Amount of money you spend for 1000 impressions
- **Clicks:** Number of times that someone clicks on your ad
- **CTR (click-through rate):** Percentage of people responding to your ad
- **CPC (cost per click):** Cost you are paying per click/action
- **Leads:** Number of people that have signed up to your database
- **LPC (landing page conversion):** Percentage of people who take action after seeing your landing page
- **CPL (cost per lead):** The cost you are paying for each new lead

Traffic ads

To drive people to your website to engage with a piece of

content (e.g., a blog). It is literally that simple; the platform will show your ad to people who are most likely to click and go to your website.

Engagement ads

To get more people to see and engage with your Facebook post or page. You can create ads that:

- Get more eyes on your posts (**Post Engagement**)
- Promote your page (**Page Likes**)
- Get people to claim an offer on your page (**Offer Claims**)
- Raise attendance at an event on your page (**Event Responses**)

This is one of my favourite ad strategies. It's like putting a billboard in front of your ideal client until such time they are ready to take some action with you.

Video views ads

To get more people to view your video content. The ad channel will show your video to more people who like to watch video.

Lead generation ads

To drive more leads based on people interested in your brand or business.

> **WARNING**
> The data supplied is the same data (i.e., name, phone, and email) as when the Facebook user joined, so it could be incorrect. The cost is generally lower than conversion, but the quality could be lower, too.

Conversion ads

To drive people to your website to fill in a form. This is my preferred choice over a lead generation ad, but as with everything in marketing, it's a test, so figure out what works for you.

Facebook pixel

The Facebook pixel is code that you embed into your website which links visitors' onsite behaviour to their Facebook profile. The sync between your website and their Facebook profile enables you to retarget those individuals with relevant ads. Also, it can be used to track the actions individuals take when they return to the website (i.e., submitting an enquiry).

You know when you look for a holiday online and then your Facebook feed is full of holiday adverts? Or you look at a pair of trainers or visit ASOS and then you're followed with ads for similar products? That is the Facebook pixel at work.

Facebook campaign

Can contain several Ad Sets and has a unique campaign objective. Your campaign is basically just a container to help you better organize your advertising. The only attribute of the campaign is the objective you want to reach with it.

So, if you want to 1) drive sales to your website and 2) increase the number of likes on your Facebook page, you'll have to create two campaigns, one for each objective. The ad type is usually the campaign type:

1. Traffic
2. Engagement
3. Video view
4. Lead generation
5. Conversion

Facebook ad set

Also known as your audience. Can include multiple ads and has a unique audience, budget, schedule, bidding, and placement. Ad sets are also the best units to use for Facebook A/B testing – remember to always place all the variations inside different ad sets.

Ad sets include:

- Age
- Sex
- Interests
- Job titles
- Books/magazines
- Demographics

You use these to narrow down the people you want to see your ad.

> **A/B Testing**
> Also known as split testing, this is a marketing experiment where you split your audience to test a few variations of a campaign and determine which performs better. In other words, you can show version A of a piece of marketing content to one half of your audience, and version B to another.

Facebook ad

This is the smallest part of your campaign. The ad itself can have different URLs, could be an image or a video. It also contains the "ad copy" (i.e., the words in your ad). Let's visualize it to make it rookie-proof:

1. Ad text
2. Ad image (could be replaced by a video)
3. Headline (ACTIVE.MORTGAGE)
4. Link description (Book your mortgage strategy call today)
5. Button (Contact us)

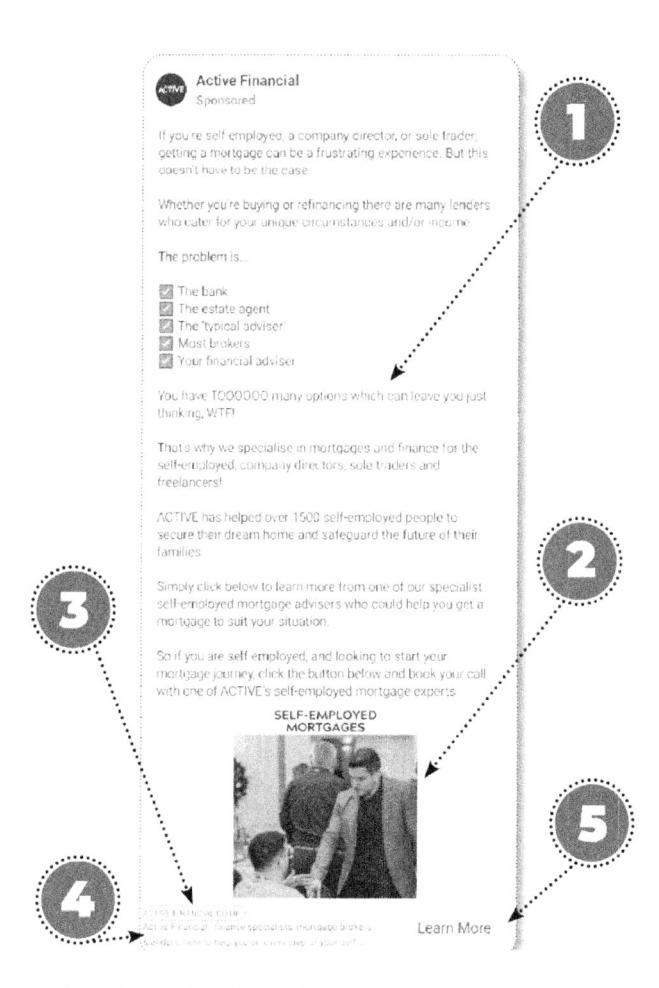

Facebook ad daily budget

This is the amount you spend on delivering your ads every day during your campaign. When you set your daily budget, you're telling Facebook to get you roughly your daily budget's worth of results.

When I am running an engagement campaign, I can spend as little as £3.00 to £5.00 every day to show my ad to my ideal client.

Some days, when Facebook spots high-potential

opportunities, it may spend up to 25% more than your daily budget (and then lower the spend on the low-potential days). When you select the daily budget, your daily ad spend could look like a set of curves. Don't worry, that's completely normal and means that Facebook's auto-optimising your ad delivery (which is a good thing).

Here's an example of my ads so you can see the kind of results we get (if you're unable to see the detail in the image, you can download it here:

https://www.garydas.com/facebook-ad-data/

- 946 Leads in a month
- £1,578.79 monthly spend
- Average £1.66 Cost per Lead
- 1% conversion = 9 deals
- Average Sale = £2,768 (total of mortgage, insurance, and fee from my brokerage)
- Total Sales = £24,912

My Facebook Strategy

I mainly run two types of ads, each on a £5+ per day budget.

1. An engagement ad which we will run 365 days a

year. This is my billboard keeping me in front of my ideal client. We will test a variety of content at different times for 1-2 months; for example, we might test an image and then switch it out for a video of varying lengths. The key is calling out our specific niche.
2. A conversion ad driving people to download my eBook. Then, within 24 hours of the download, my team will typically contact the lead to confirm receipt, interest and/or follow up. This is the start of a relationship to solve their problems.

Facebook Key Advantages

The first advantage I love with Facebook is the ability to target anyone who has liked, commented, or shared my engagement ad (1 above) with my conversion ad (2). This improves the quality of the lead and improves our conversion from lead to sale.

The second huge advantage of Facebook is the ability to create lookalike audiences. When you import your client data or choose people who have downloaded your eBook, for example, Facebook can find similar people based on their demographic and interests. They are easy to create and implement, making them extremely powerful for finding high-converting leads.

I follow these exact same principles and methods as above for my other businesses. When you test, measure and know your numbers well enough, you can build a predictable lead generation machine, and, unlike when I used to buy leads, you are in complete control.

Step 4 Actions

1. Set up your Google My Business (GMB) account.
2. Choose your high-value free gift to give to your leads.
3. Create a landing page and thank you page or your free gift.
4. Set up an email sequence to build value after delivery.
5. Learn an ad platform and then drive ads to your landing page.

Notes

STEP 5
Sales Strategies

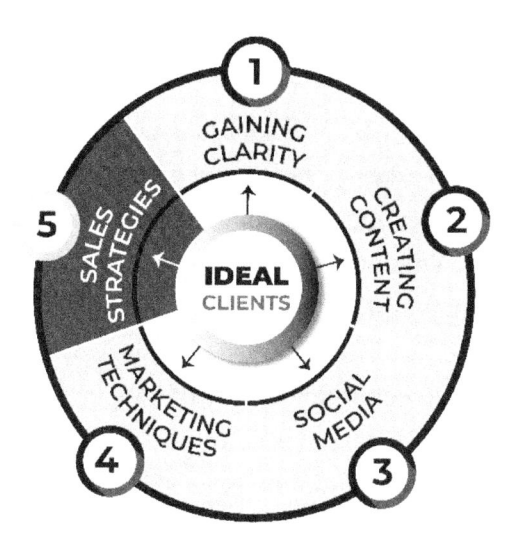

Since starting my marketing journey in 2016, I've had a consistent focus on generating leads for my businesses. Much like planting a seed, watering it, nurturing, and harvesting it, the longer you play the game, the better you get and the more results you see.

When you implement everything in this book, your

clients come to your pre-sold; the need to sell on the phone is reduced because they have built up so much know, like, and trust with you that they have no desire to work with anyone else.

The best enquiry for my business is one that rings my HQ, messages me on social media, or contacts us saying:

1. I watched a video online
2. That led me to the 7 Mistakes eBook
3. Your emails drove me to purchase The Self-Employed Mortgage Guide from Amazon
4. I have put XYZ right
5. I have all my documents ready for you, where do I send them?

But the hardest part of business is getting your lead on to the phone. In a fast-paced world where attention spans are getting shorter and Amazon keeps making the buying process faster with one-click purchases and simple upsells, you need to make sure that you can convert your conversations.

Being able to communicate, build rapport, and sell online and over the phone is so important for you and your business. There are entire books on sales and it's an area, especially for advisers, that is very specific. My belief is you need to continually sharpen your axe.

> *"If I only had an hour to chop down a tree, I would spend the first 45 minutes sharpening my axe."*
> *– Abraham Lincoln.*

Sales conversations

The modern buyer is no longer receptive to outdated tricks and hard sell tactics. Sales conversations need to add value from the start, much like your social media effort. You need to clearly differentiate your capabilities and build a clear vision of a proposition uniquely placed to address the lead's requirements.

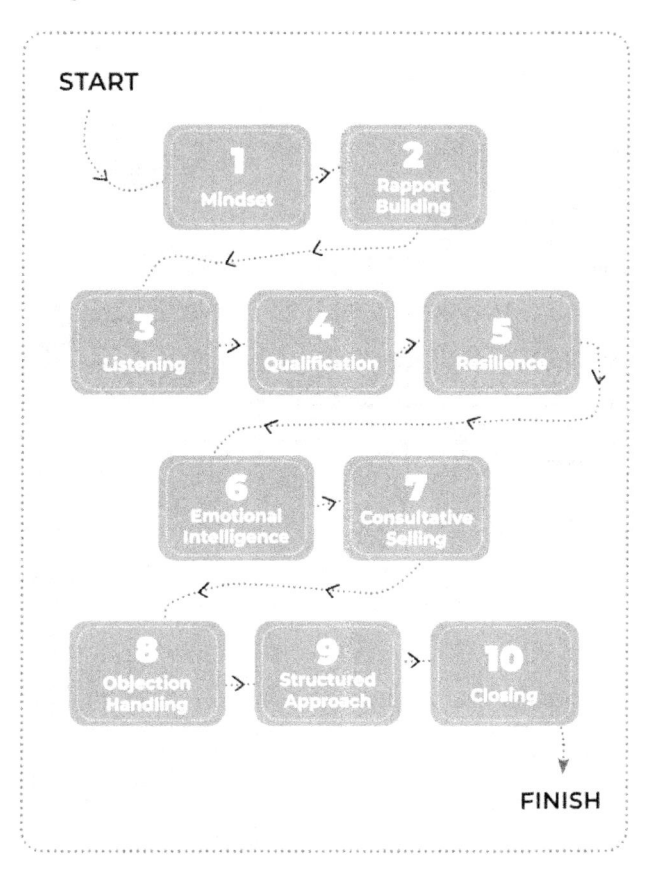

START

1. Mindset
2. Rapport Building
3. Listening
4. Qualification
5. Resilience
6. Emotional Intelligence
7. Consultative Selling
8. Objection Handling
9. Structured Approach
10. Closing

FINISH

To make the most of your sales conversations, here are my top ten tips for closing more deals, from getting in the right mindset before the call to applying emotional intelligence and building rapport.

1. Mindset

Being well-prepared for your sales conversation before you even pick up the phone is critical to your success. This includes researching your lead in advance through social media, news articles, or online resources, preparing the message you want to get across, and setting clear objectives for what you need to achieve from the call. Failing to prepare is preparing to fail, so planning should also include anticipating setbacks and objections raised.

2. Rapport building

For your sales conversation to move your lead along the purchase path, they need to feel confident and trust that you have value to offer. Rapport is the first stage in building that trust and establishing credibility. A positive, open attitude, strong listening skills, and a genuine interest in their needs are just some of the key requisites to building good rapport.

3. Listening

Effective communication is like tennis; a back-and-forth exchange rather than a one-sided pitch, so listening skills are critical. Understand, repeat back, stay open, remain curious, and learn about the problems, challenges and needs of your lead. Not only will this establish a genuine connection, but it also creates a platform on which to position your proposition and present a compelling solution.

4. Qualification

You need to qualify your leads fast, it needs to happen at the start of all conversations. If you have done your marketing correctly and spoken directly to your ideal client, then leads should be coming to you pre-qualified. If a lead isn't a good fit or they don't have an appetite to buy, it is a waste of your time and theirs in terms of the sales process. Don't be afraid to ask direct questions to establish their role from the outset and avoid assumptions based on job title, those vary from company to company and may not guarantee the lead is the right fit for you.

5. Resilience

Not every conversation will go as planned and developing resilience is a core part of being in sales. Rather than feeling defeated, use setbacks as an opportunity to learn, reassess, and adapt your approach so you increase the likelihood of future success. If you then re-engage and are able to overcome your buyer's objections, you will have increased your credibility and strengthened their trust in you. And if they aren't ready to buy, you can redirect your efforts to the right leads.

6. Emotional intelligence

An awareness of how you communicate and the ability to put yourself in the buyer's shoes will always improve the effectiveness of a sales conversation. Listening, showing empathy, demonstrating that you really understand their pain, and acknowledging the challenges and issues they face will build trust and enable you to position your solution appropriately and with credibility.

7. Consultative selling

As a salesperson, start by discovering a lead's concerns, wants, and needs to influence their buying decisions. Effective sales conversations should provide an open dialogue that explores the customers' problems, fears, and desires and builds an understanding of their specific needs and the outcomes they want to achieve. Without that level of understanding, it is impossible to identify and provide the right solution.

8. Objection handling

Objections are inevitable in the sales process but recognising them as an opportunity to better understand the customer and their desires is crucial to overall success. Objections mean that your buyer isn't convinced that you understand their issue or that your solution offers an effective solution. This means you need to step back, regroup, and re-angle your key messages to create a more compelling case.

9. Structured approach

Use frameworks to support a consistent approach to your sales conversations. Whether defining your target lead, specifying qualification criteria using BANT (Budget, Need, Authority, and Timeline), or adopting the five W's (who, what, when, where and why) to gather in-depth customer insight, a structured approach will make your efforts more focused and consistent.

10. Closing

If you have built genuine rapport with a lead, handled their objections well, and communicated the value of your proposition effectively, closing the sale should be a natural next step for both parties. If you have addressed all their concerns and they are convinced you offer an effective solution, there is no reason why you shouldn't feel confident asking how they would like to move forward or if they would like you to draw up the necessary paperwork. If you feel uncertain or fearful, you need to reassess.

Sell the solution not the product

"When you sell a man a book you don't sell just twelve ounces of paper and ink and glue — you sell him a whole new life. Love and friendship and humour and ships at sea by night — there's all heaven and earth in a book, a real book." — Christopher Morley

"Don't sell life insurance. Sell what life insurance can do." — Ben Feldman

"It isn't that they can't see the solution. It's that they can't see the problem." — G K Chesterton

"The best salespeople know that their expertise can become their enemy in selling. At the moment, they are tempted to tell the buyer what "he needs to do," they instead offer a story about a peer of the buyer." — Mike Bosworth, Author of *Solution Selling*

The above quotes have one thing in common, they highlight that when it comes to selling a service or a product, the focus should be on selling the solution to a problem. You can often get lost in the process and lose sight of what is actually important. Do you buy products, or do you buy the benefits that purchasing a certain product brings? If the solution you are providing really works, helps people and they are satisfied, then why wouldn't you sell with conviction and confidence?

The fortune is in the follow up
Too many business owners give up too early. If you have taken the time, energy and effort to work out your niche, produce consistent content, leverage social media, build out a marketing funnel (including your eBook, landing page, thank you page, and email sequences) and managed to get your lead on a call, don't fall at the last hurdle by not taking the time to follow up.

You don't need to harass them or constantly bombard the person with calls, emails, WhatsApp and text messages, but you must use a customer relationship management (CRM) system to maintain contact and keep following up until such time they are ready to buy from you.

As you can see below, 80% of sales are made between the 5th and the 12th follow up. The timescale maybe over one month or even a year, so keeping in contact is essential to build your business for the future.

SALES STATISTICS

48%	Of sales people never follow up with a prospect
25%	Of sales people make a second contact and stop
12%	Of sales people only make three contacts and stop
10%	Of sales people make more then three contacts
2%	Of sales are made on the first contact
3%	Of sales are made on the second contact
5%	Of sales are made on the third contact
10%	Of sales are made on the fourth contact
80%	Of sales are made on the fifth to twelfth contact

Sales is serving   Source: National Sales Executive Association

Sales is serving

Sales is a part of life; whether you are selling your children on cleaning their teeth every night (a painful process in my house) or selling your services to a high-ticket client, sales is not dirty or something to be ashamed of. Sales is part of life and a skill, like marketing, that you will need throughout your business journey.

Step 5 Actions

1. Create a sales script that focuses on solutions
2. Pick up the phone and speak to people more often
3. Set up a CRM system to automate your sales process as much as possible
4. Follow up with leads consistently over a long period of time to increase conversions

Notes

Summary

I hope you have enjoyed the Lead Generation Guide. It has the evergreen elements I have developed from a six-figure investment into marketing and sales skills development. If you want a lead generation strategy that will consistently deliver leads into your business, allow you to have good conversations with qualified prospects, and increase your income then, focus on developing this simple strategy:

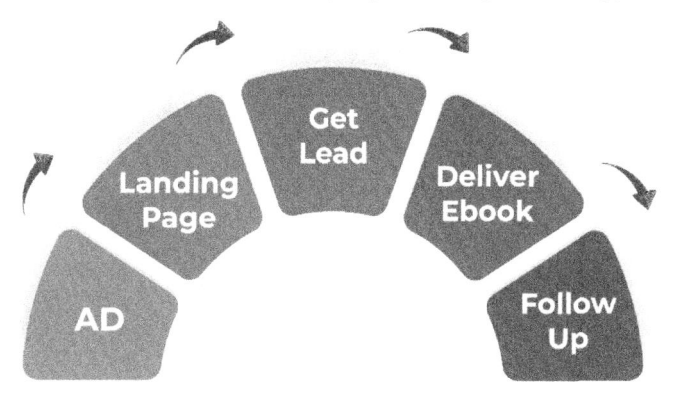

- 1 niche
- 1 content marketing method
- 1 landing page

- 1 thank you page
- 1 lead capture method
- 1 email sequence
- 1 ad (Facebook, Google, YouTube, Instagram, TikTok… and make sure you learn the platform)

What To Do Next

At this stage, we don't know each other, and I don't know where you are in the AIDA model. But I do know you have read this book because you need help with your lead generation and want to increase your sales. So, here are some options to illustrate everything I have outlined here for you and so we can, hopefully, get to know each other better.

The PRO Podcast
With over 200 episodes and 200,000 downloads, I document my journey, share my personal and business challenges, along with the lessons on the way.

- On all major channels – Apple, Spotify, Alexa, YouTube etc.
- For anyone wanting to be a PRO.
- In my 2019 launch, this reached number one worldwide in business and marketing.

www.garydas.com/podcast

Connect with me on social media
- @garydas
- Send me a DM and let me know what you liked about the book.
- I look forward to starting a conversation, building a relationship, and growing together.
- Don't forget to share a picture of the book on your social media using #leadgenerationguide

Grab my eBook
How to Generate Leads for Less: A 4-step process to generate free leads from social media in just 15-30 minutes per day, including 30 tips to generate leads in 30 days.

https://30tips.theleadgenerationguide.co.uk

Take the quiz
Benchmark your current lead generation performance and identify opportunities for attracting your ideal client and increasing your sales:

https://scorecard.theleadgenerationguide.co.uk

About the Author

Gary Das is an entrepreneur, bestselling author, speaker, lover of fitness, husband, and father of four. He became self-employed in 2006 and spent his first ten years buying leads from third-party companies, before realising he had built a business he *hated* due to spending £20,000 per month on such low-quality leads.

Since 2016, Gary has been on a journey of discovery and learning and has found a passion for marketing and sales. He has now built multiple successful businesses in a variety of service-based industries and teaches other self-employed people how to generate leads, increase sales, and maximise profit so they can live a lifestyle they love.

The Lead Generation Guide is based on what Gary has done and continues to work for him when it comes to starting, growing, and scaling his businesses.

Gary has generated thousands of leads in a variety of industries and the methods in this book have made his businesses more than £5m in just seven years with very little marketing spend. Year on year, the compound effect of content and social media increases his return on lead generation investment.

"The only reason I have been able achieve my level of success is because of my wife Ayesha, who believes in me, challenges me, and supports (most) of my decisions like no one else does.

I have made a large number of mistakes in business, confidently get things wrong, and share the lessons with other entrepreneurs on my YouTube channel and Podcast, so you don't make the same mistakes, too.

A massive thank you for taking the time to read and digest this book."

For more information about Gary, visit www.garydas.com

Printed in Great Britain
by Amazon